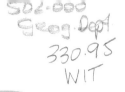

ENVIRONMENT &
PEOPLE
INTEGRATED
COURSE
SUPPLEMENTS

DEVELOPMENT, DISPARITY *and* DEPENDENCE

A Study of the Asian Pacific Region

Michael Witherick

Series Editor:
Michael Witherick

Stanley Thornes (Publishers) Ltd

First published in 1998 by:
Stanley Thornes (Publishers) Ltd
Ellenborough House
Wellington Street
CHELTENHAM GL50 1YW
England

98 99 00 01 02 / 10 9 8 7 6 5 4 3 2 1

A catalogue record for this book is available from the British Library.

ISBN 0-7487-3185-7

Printed and bound in Great Britain by Martins The Printers Ltd., Berwick upon Tweed

Acknowledgements

The author and publishers would like to thank the following for permission to reproduce copyright material:

The Financial Times: Fig. 4.4 (map and tables), 15 December 1996. Fig. 4.5, 'The role of women' article by Robert Taylor, 15 November 1996. Fig. 4.6 (maps and charts), 10 October 1996. Fig. 4.7 (map and charts), 18 February 1997. Fig. 4.10 'The growing bond between Hong Kong and China' (map and text), 19 March 1996. Fig. 5.5 (map and charts), 5 December 1996. Fig. 5.8 'Sony in Asia' (map and text), 15 November 1995; The Institute of British Geographers: Fig. 4.9 (map) from M. Witherick and D. A. Pinter in M. Williams (ed.) (1990) *Wetlands: A threatened landscape*, Blackwell; *The Times*: Fig. 4.5 'Economic hangover turning an Asian tiger. . .' article by Oliver August, 8 January 1997. Fig. 6.7 'Britons start tours to North Korea' article by Harvey Elliott, 22 January 1997, all © Times Newspapers Limited, 1997; UNICEF: Fig. 6.8; The World Bank: Fig. 6.4 (charts), from *Cambodia: From Recovery to Sustained Development* (1996) (Report no. 15593-KH).

Ecoscene, Figs. 7.2, 7.8; Science Photo Library, Fig. 3.2; Travel Ink, Figs. 1.2, 3.1, 4.8.

Every effort has been made to contact copyright holders. The publishers apologise to anyone whose rights have been inadvertently overlooked, and will be happy to rectify any errors or omissions.

Contents

Development, disparities and the Asian Pacific region

SECTION A

Introduction

The aim of this book is to explore in more depth and detail some of the content of the Economic Activity module in *Environment and People* (**E & P**). The intent is also to examine one of the Integrating Themes – **IT4 Sustainability** – and one of the Integrated Places – **IP1 Tokyo and Japan**.

The key word throughout this book is **development**. For this reason, it is vital that we start with a clear understanding of what it means. The problem is that there is no universally agreed definition. The word is used in a range of different subjects: from urban studies to human physiology, from photography to mathematics. It could easily take a whole book to explore the various meanings of this one word in those different contexts. Even within geography, sociology and economics – subjects sharing the same broad view of development – there is debate as to what exactly is involved.

In this book, any discussion of what development means must necessarily be brief. The best that can be done is to isolate what in geographical studies are generally accepted as its main characteristics. Hopefully, this will provide a sound starting-point.

SECTION B

What is development? (E & P 30.1)

Geography is about how places and people differ over the Earth's surface. In geography, the following are widely accepted as development characteristics :
- Development is a process of change operating over time; it is evolutionary in character.
- The process involves exploiting potential and moving towards more advanced states.
- Development varies spatially; its precise character and speed vary from place to place, creating differences between and within countries.
- It is a complex process, with many different strands – broadly these may be classified as cultural, economic, environmental, political, social and technological.

The debate in geography about development is to do with the relative importance of these different strands. On the one hand, there are those who emphasise the importance of economic factors. They argue that economic growth is the powerhouse of development. The wealth it creates drives progress in all the other strands.

In contrast to this view, there are those who believe that development is really about achieving greater social justice within and between countries. For them, development is a process of satisfying basic human needs, improving the quality of life and allowing people to fulfil their potential. Economic growth is seen as having the ability to both hinder and help achieve those goals. It can both widen and narrow the gap between rich and poor.

This book inclines to the former view of development. Economic growth is taken as the major thrust of development, but working in partnership with technology and enterprise The relationship is a reciprocal one. Enterprise and advances in technology help economic growth. At the same time, economic growth leads to more enterprise and new technology. However, in seeing the economic and technological aspects as the core of development, we should not ignore the importance of parallel advances and outcomes in other fields.

Figure 1.1
The development cable

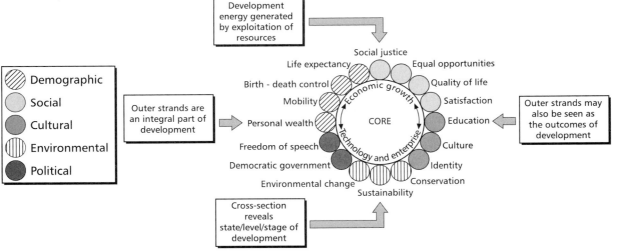

Perhaps it might help to draw an analogy. Development may be likened to an electric cable (**1.1**). Through it passes the power by which countries and societies progress from primitive to more advanced states. The core of the cable is an alloy of economic growth, technology and enterprise. An integral part of that cable is an outer casing woven from many different strands. Whilst the general specification of the cable is basically the same for all countries and regions, its 'carrying capacity' (or wattage) can vary. A high-capacity cable allows more power to pass through and can therefore support faster development. But the capacity of the cable can vary over time. Cutting the cable at any point along its length will reveal a cross-section. The collective condition of the components so exposed constitutes what is often termed the **stage** (or **state** or **level**) **of development**.

By now you may be wondering what generates the power that flows along the development cable. The short answer is the exploitation of **resources** (natural and human); this is development's vital fuel. It feeds in at the plug-end of the cable. The amount of energy entering the core at any time depends on two things: the rate and scale of resource exploitation, and the cable's carrying capacity. Pulses of acceleration and deceleration in the rate of development result from changes in these two variables.

The increasing global concern about the rate and scale at which natural resources are being used is an acknowledgement of their fundamental importance to development. There is also a concern that development needs to become much more sustainable. **Sustainable development** has been defined as 'a wise use of resources and appropriate technology that can be sustained without adversely affecting the natural environment. Development that meets the needs of today without compromising the ability of future generations to meet their own needs' (J. Small and M. Witherick (1995) *A Modern Dictionary of Geography*, Edward Arnold). So the emphasis is very much on a sparing use of **non-renewable resources** and a sensible use of **renewable resources**. At the end of this book we will return to this issue of sustainable development and try to answer these key questions:

- Can sustainable development be realised, or is it just a utopian idea?
- To what extent has sustainable development been put into practice within the Asian Pacific region?

Let us sum up so far. For the purposes of this book, development is defined as the process by which countries and societies advance. That progress is driven primarily by the use of resources in tandem with new technology and enterprise. The process can operate at a range of speeds and can have many different outcomes that affect both people and their environment.

Review

1 Identify the different strands of development illustrated in **1.2**.

2 a Define the term sustainable development.
  b Give three examples to illustrate your definition.

Figure 1.2 Development and some of its outcomes

How to measure development (E & P 30.2)

We are all aware that the level of development varies between and within countries. But is it possible to measure or to be precise about such variations? What might seem a simple task is immediately complicated by the multi-strand nature of development (**1.1** and **1.2**). However, if we stick to the definition of development given in the previous section, then measurement is going to be mainly about the economic and technological aspects, particularly the former.

Economic measures

Probably the most widely used and accepted measure of development at an international level is **GNP per capita**. A nation's **gross national product** is the total value of its economic production in one year. It takes into account the production of goods, the provision of services, profits from overseas investments and the money earned in the country by foreign people and businesses. By calculating it on a per capita basis, population differences between countries are neutralised. Figures for 1995 published by the World Bank showed that GNP per capita ranged from $80 in Mozambique to $41 210 in Luxembourg. The figure for the UK was $18 700.

GDP per capita is another economic measure. A country's **gross domestic product** refers only to the total value of goods and services produced there during one year. Since it excludes overseas earnings, it tends to undervalue the capacities of the more advanced economies, which are typically heavily involved in offshore activities. This is illustrated by the statistics in **1.5**.

Both measures – GNP and GDP – have their problems. First, it is frequently the case that data are not readily available for all countries in any one year. Secondly, such vital statistics are sometimes 'massaged' – reported inaccurately – mainly for political reasons.

By looking at the GNP or GDP figures recorded for a country over a number of years, it is possible to work out an average annual rate of growth. Such a figure can give a crude indication of the rate of development and can also be used to compare countries. To be really useful, however, the calculation of the average rate of annual growth needs to take into account the rate of inflation. A high rate of inflation can easily make the annual rate of growth in GNP per capita seem much more impressive than it really is. When inflation is taken into account, economists refer to **real growth**. Between 1985 and 1995, one of the highest rates of real growth, 8 per cent per annum, was recorded by China. In contrast, the former Soviet Republic of Georgia experienced an average annual decline of 17 per cent.

Technological measures

The amount of energy consumed per head of population is another widely used indicator of development. It is based on the argument that many of the advances in technology that are part of development increase energy consumption. Clearly this is often the case with progress in transport

Review

3 Explain why it is better to express GNP, GDP and other measures of development in per capita terms.

4 Suggests reasons why a government might 'massage' the statistics about its development.

5 Can you think of any other technological indicators that might be used in the measurement of development?

6 Figure **1.3** shows some social indicators of development. Can you think of any other aspects of the quality of life that might be taken into account?

(more, faster and larger vehicles) and manufacturing (more sophisticated machinery). Equally, it is so with home improvements like central heating, air conditioning and the greater use of modern gadgetry. However, there is growing public concern about the use of non-renewable energy sources, and more responsible governments are trying to achieve a much more efficient use of energy. Success here ultimately lowers per capita energy consumption. Clearly, this complicates what used to be seen as a simple correlation with development. So today, a falling rate of per capita energy consumption might be seen as an indicator of the most advanced countries. In 1995 per capita energy consumption in the world ranged from 7kg coal equivalent in the Solomon Islands to 33 843kg in the Virgin Islands, USA; the figure for the UK was 3 772kg. (**E & P Fig. 27.4**)

Social measures

Although this book adopts a very economic view of development, it is worth indicating the sorts of measures used by those who emphasise that development should be measured in terms of the quality of life and the satisfaction of human needs. Possible indicators fall into three fairly obvious groupings (1.3).

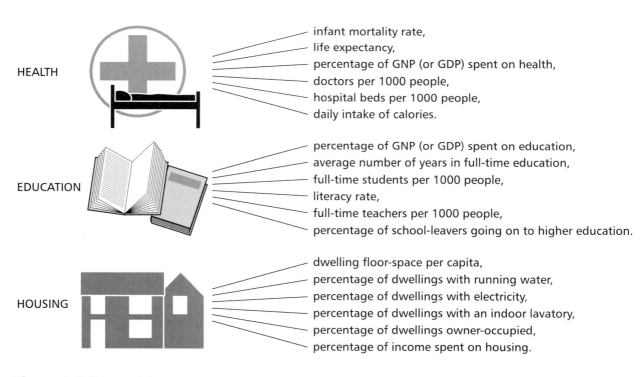

HEALTH
- infant mortality rate,
- life expectancy,
- percentage of GNP (or GDP) spent on health,
- doctors per 1000 people,
- hospital beds per 1000 people,
- daily intake of calories.

EDUCATION
- percentage of GNP (or GDP) spent on education,
- average number of years in full-time education,
- full-time students per 1000 people,
- literacy rate,
- full-time teachers per 1000 people,
- percentage of school-leavers going on to higher education.

HOUSING
- dwelling floor-space per capita,
- percentage of dwellings with running water,
- percentage of dwellings with electricity,
- percentage of dwellings with an indoor lavatory,
- percentage of dwellings owner-occupied,
- percentage of income spent on housing.

Figure 1.3 Some social indicators of development

Multivariate measures

Given that development is recognised as a multi-strand process (**1.1**), it follows that serious consideration should be given to devising some sort of composite index. To date, two such multivariate measures have been widely adopted.

The Physical Quality of Life Index (PQLI)

This index involves taking the averages of three measures: literacy, life expectancy and infant mortality. Each is scaled from 0 to 100 (from worst to best). The composite index is then calculated by averaging the three indicators, giving equal weight to each of them. A PQLI of 77 has been set as the threshold of 'basic human needs'. Currently, around two-thirds of the world's population lives below this level. (**E & P 30.3**)

The Human Development Index (HDI)

This was devised in 1990. Like the PQLI it takes into account three variables which are given equal weighting: income per capita, adult literacy and life expectancy. The HDI takes the highest and lowest values recorded for each variable by the countries of the world. The interval between them is given a value of 1 and then the value for each country is scored on a scale of 0 to 1 (from worst to best). The HDI is the average score of the three variables and so too is expressed as a value between 0 and 1. The wealthy developed countries have an index approaching 0.999 and the poorer countries range down to less than 0.300. (**E & P 30.5**)

Review

7 a Which of the two measures – PQLI and HDI – do you think is better? Give your reasons.
b Look at **E & P 30.3** and **30.5**. To what extent do they show similar patterns?

SECTION D

The Asian Pacific region – a diversity of nations

The Asian Pacific region comprises 15 countries that face or lie close to the western shores of the Pacific Ocean (**1.4**). For the purposes of this study, the region does not include either the Russian Republic or Papua New Guinea. There are strong contrasts between the member countries – not only in terms of their economies (**1.5**), but also:

- in size (area and population), as between China and Singapore (**1.6**);
- in latitude, as between Hokkaido, the northernmost island of Japan, and Timor, the southernmost island of Indonesia (**1.4**);
- in location, as between inland Laos, peninsular Malaysia and insular Taiwan;
- in politics, as between socialist North Korea and capitalist South Korea;
- in prosperity, as between Japan and Vietnam (**1.5**).

The World Bank sees these countries, as indeed all countries, as falling into one of three categories based on GNP per capita (**1.4** and **1.5**). In the case of the second grouping, a distinction is often made between lower middle-income and upper middle-income economies. Of the 15 nations in the Asian Pacific region, only one is classified as high income. The remainder are seen as falling within the poorer global 'South'. (**E & P 30.1**)

One vital point to be made here is that disparities in development occur at a range of spatial scales. Within each of the countries of the Asian Pacific region, no matter what their overall level of development, the development is not evenly spread. There will be **cores** and **peripheries**. (**E&P 30.3**)

Figure 1.4
The Asian Pacific region

Figure 1.5 The economic grouping of Asian Pacific countries

Economic grouping		GNP (1995) ($bn)	GNP per capita (1995) ($)	GDP per capita (1994) ($)	Real growth (1985-95) (% per year)	Energy consumption per capita (tonnes)
High income	Japan	4 963.6	39 640	36 863	3.6	4.74
Higher middle-income	Singapore	79.8	26 690	24 024	6.1	8.50
	Hong Kong	142.3	22 990	21 752	5.3	2.29
	Taiwan	263.3	12 440	11 415	7.0	no data
	Brunei	?3.0	?9 000	no data	1.0	2.18
	South Korea	338.1	7 760	8 616	8.1	3.19
Lower middle-income	Malaysia	78.3	3 890	3 668	5.7	1.80
	Thailand	159.6	2 740	2 131	8.4	0.89
	Philippines	71.9	1 050	973	1.6	0.40
	Indonesia	190.1	980	765	4.8	0.38
Low income	China	744.9	620	425	6.5	0.35
	Laos	1.7	350	no data	2.1	0.04
	Cambodia	2.7	270	no data	7.5	no data
	Vietnam	17.6	240	no data	4.8	0.12
	North Korea	no data	no data	no data	–8.0	0.06

	Area (km²)	Total population (millions)	Urban population (% tot. pop)	Population change (1990–95) (% per year)	Life expectancy (years)	
					M	F
China	9 596 960	1 185.0	28	1.3	69	73
Indonesia	1 904 570	198.6	33	2.1	61	65
Thailand	513 120	53.4	19	0.4	65	69
Japan	377 800	125.2	77	0.3	76	82
Vietnam	331 690	74.6	20	2.3	62	66
Malaysia	329 750	20.2	51	2.4	69	73
Philippines	300 000	67.2	51	1.5	63	70
Laos	236 800	4.9	20	3.5	50	53
Cambodia	181 040	9.2	19	2.9	50	52
North Korea	120 540	23.9	60	1.9	66	72
South Korea	99 020	45.1	77	1.1	67	73
Taiwan	36 000	21.1	75	0.7	72	78
Brunei	5 770	0.3	58	1.6	74	77
Hong Kong	1 040	6.2	94	0.5	75	80
Singapore	618	3.0	100	2.1	72	77

Figure 1.6 Geographic and demographic features of Asian Pacific countries (1995)

Global shifts and the rise of the Asian Pacific region

1.7 looks at the Asian Pacific region in terms of its shares of four global measures. The upward trend in all measures over the 25-year period gives an indication of its dynamic or **sunrise** character.

	1970	1995
GNP		
Exports	11	29
Imports	13	25
Stock markets	2	9
Energy consumption	10	19

Figure 1.7 The Asian Pacific region's shares of global measures (1970–95)

From the beginning of the Industrial Revolution in the mid-18th century to the middle of the 20th century, it was the countries fringing the North Atlantic that constituted the main focus of world development. Since the Second World War, however, as the distribution of economic growth within North America has shifted from the East Coast to America's West Coast, so the global pendulum has swung towards the North Pacific. This has led economists to talk of the 'dawn of a Pacific era'. The countries rimming the North Pacific are now part of an upwardly-mobile region. Although the USA is unchallenged as the most powerful of those nations, its weight and that of Canada are now counterbalanced by collective developments on the Asian side. Indeed, this sector – the Asian Pacific region – is very much in the ascendant.

Review

8 Which of the four measures in **1.7** do you think gives the best indication of the region's sunrise status? Give reasons for your choice.

TRINITY GRAMMAR SCHOOL

Key questions

In the next six chapters we will take a closer look at the 15 countries of the Asian Pacific region and the individual contributions they have made to its sunrise status. From these case studies, it is hoped to find answers to some fundamental questions about development:

- Is the character of development the same in all countries? Is the development cable everywhere the same?
- Do all countries progress through the same sequence of development? Does the cable create a common development pathway?
- Why are some countries more successful than others? Why are there disparities in development both between and within countries?

Because Japan is the leading economy of the region, the analysis of its development warrants rather more space than that of the other countries. But also because of this leadership, you will find that all the subsequent analyses look at the links which those countries have with Japan. In this sense, then, the 'Japanese connection', as we might term it, is an important theme running through the book.

Enquiry

1 For any one country in the Asian Pacific Region, find out:
   a its main sources of energy;
   b its main consumers of energy;
   c the extent to which it relies on imported energy;
   d what is being done to reduce energy consumption.

2 a Using the data in **1.5**, divide the 15 countries into four groups based on (i) real growth (1985–95) and (ii) per capita energy consumption.
   b To what extent do your two groupings coincide with the economic groupings?
   c Suggests reasons for any differences that there might be.

3 a Referring to the data in **1.6**, are you able to generalise about the demographic characteristics of the countries that make up each of the four economic groupings?
   b If your answer is 'yes', state what those generalisations are.
   c If your answer is 'no', suggest reasons for the lack of correlation.

4 Using the data in **1.6**:
   a calculate the mean population density in each country;
   b rank the countries;
   c draw a choropleth map to represent your mean values;
   d write a short account of the distribution pattern shown by your map.

5 a Find out what development means in:
   - photography;
   - mathematics;
   - human physiology;
   - urbanisation.
   b Are your four meanings the same?
   c To what extent do they embody the same basic idea as the geographer's definition given in this chapter?

CHAPTER 2

Japan: from ruins to world power

Introduction

Japan's status as a global superstar and as the leading economy of the Asian Pacific region is undisputed. Since 1968 it has ranked as the world's second most powerful economy, after the USA. Japan's emergence as a front-runner in terms of economic development is quite remarkable, bearing in mind three facts:

- it possesses few mineral and energy resources;
- it did not start to industrialise until the second half of the 19th century – nearly 100 years later than the UK;
- its physical and industrial infrastructure lay in ruins at the end of the Second World War (1945).

So the obvious question to be asked is: what has been the secret of Japan's success? In particular, what factors enabled Japan to achieve the spectacular change from ruins to riches within a 20-year span during the post-war period?

Figure 2.1 Growth in the Japanese economy (1950–95)

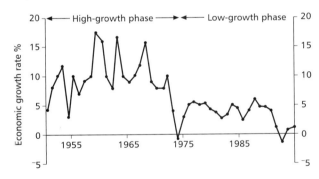

First, though, we need to look at two indicators of what is often referred to as Japan's 'economic miracle': the annual rate of economic growth (based on GNP) and shifts in the sectoral balance of the economy. These measures are widely used in studies of development. Their advantage is that they are reasonably consistent over time. Their definition does not change and they are not affected by inflation. Thus they allow a reliable monitoring of change.

Review

1 What is the difference between GNP and GDP?

Economic growth rates

So far as movement in the economic growth rate is concerned, it is possible to define two distinct phases – high growth (between 1951 and 1973) and low growth (from 1974 onwards) (2.1). During the former phase, the economic growth rate averaged about 10 per cent per annum, whilst in the latter it has fallen to around 3 per cent. The first phase was brought to an abrupt halt by the 1973 Oil Crisis, which profoundly shook the Japanese economy. The following year was the first of only two during the whole post-war era when the economy failed to record any growth (the other was 1993). Within both phases, particularly the former, there have been considerable oscillations in the rate of growth from year to year.

It would be easy to write Japan off on the basis of its current low rate of economic growth (**2.1**). However, growth rates need to be considered in the light of the mass of the economy. The high rates of growth during the 1960s certainly generated a huge economy. So today although the rate of growth is lower, linked to the mammoth economy that has since been consolidated, there is more actual growth than when a high rate was linked to a smaller economy. For example, in 1990, the annual growth rate was 4.8 per cent; in Malaysia it was twice that. Yet the Japanese economy grew in that one year by an amount that was twice the total value of the Malaysian economy.

A few more statistics will help put the Japanese economy into perspective. In 1995 its value was two-thirds that of the US economy, but over twice that of Germany and four times that of the UK. Even more telling was the fact that its value was more than twice that of all the other economies in the Asian Pacific region put together.

Review

2 Identify and explain the main trends shown in **2.1**.

3 Why did the Oil Crisis of 1973 so badly affect the Japanese economy?

SECTION B

Sectoral shifts

2.2 shows important shifts in the sectoral balance of the economy that have taken place since 1950. Such shifts are very much a component of development (see **Chapters 1 and 6**). There seems to be a loose relationship with the two phases just noted, in that the shifts took place at a faster rate during the high-growth phase. In the low-growth phase, there is more than a hint of levelling off.

Figure 2.2 Sectoral shifts in the Japanese economy (1950–95)

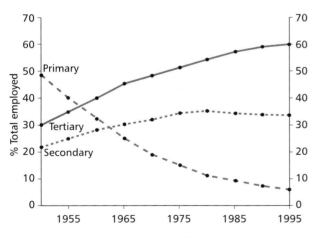

Primary sector

Undoubtedly the major change in the Japanese economy has been the decline in its primary sector, whose share of total employment has fallen from around 50 to 6 per cent (**2.2**). Whilst this sector is largely about agriculture (forestry, fishing and mining create very few jobs today), it would be wrong to interpret the curve as representing a decline in Japanese agriculture. Far from it: although agriculture is now essentially a part-time activity, and still lacking in efficiency (due mainly to the very small size of most holdings), it has significantly raised its productivity. Today, Japan produces 58 per cent of all its food requirements (this comparing with a figure of 73 per cent for the UK). Particularly important for the Japanese diet, the country is 90 per cent self-sufficient in basic foods such as rice, vegetables, fish and eggs.

These achievements in the realms of agriculture should not be understated. Although not a star performer, and somewhat protected from foreign competition, nevertheless farming has played its part in the Japanese success story.

Review

4 Identify the main trends shown in **2.2**.

Secondary sector

The secondary sector – that is, manufacturing – is widely regarded as being the powerhouse of the Japanese economy. Interestingly, of the three sectors, it is the one that has shown the least change (**2.2**). Its percentage share of employment increased only from 22 to 34 per cent over the period, and the latter figure has now applied for some 20 years.

2.2 perhaps gives the impression of a rather static sector. This is not the case. Japanese manufacturing has undergone some fundamental changes. In the early post-war period, the leading role in this sector passed from textiles to heavy industries, such as iron and steel and shipbuilding. It was these that spearheaded the high economic growth in the 1960s (**2.1**). In the low-growth phase, the processing and assembling industries have come to the fore. In the latter category, expansion has been particularly marked in the field of high-technology, such as electronics and precision equipment, and in a wide range of consumer goods, from motor cars to personal stereos.

Tertiary sector

Given the image that Japan has around the world, namely as an industrial nation, it is perhaps surprising that the most important sector is now the tertiary one – that is, providing services rather than producing goods. During the post-war period the tertiary sector's share of total employment has doubled from 30 to 60 per cent (**2.2**). In a sense, this sector is the best indicator of development and economic success. As people earn more, so they are able to spend more on services, and the sector expands. It is a **virtuous upward spiral**.

Services fall into two broad groups: commercial and social. Of the 39 million people working in the sector, roughly two-thirds have jobs in commercial services. By far the most important category here is retailing and wholesaling. Most shops in Japan are still run as family businesses; they are small and very labour-intensive. Then there is transport and communication. Japan has many more public transport services than the UK. Communications are big business in a country leading the information revolution. Next there are the millions of office jobs related to company administration, finance, insurance and real estate. Finally, there is the hotel and catering business. The current boom in leisure and recreation in Japan is making tourism a growth industry. As demand expands, so all sorts of jobs spin off, from tour guides to travel agents, and in all sorts of places, from rural hot springs to suburban theme parks.

The social services are those provided for the welfare of people. Two particularly significant categories are medical care and education. There are 1.7 million doctors, nurses, dentists, etc., and just under 1.5 million teachers. The number of jobs in social services is directly affected by the amount of money a government is willing or able to spend. The number is also influenced by the voluntary payments individuals are able or prepared to make from their income. Again, this part of the tertiary sector is a useful

Review

5 a How has the character of Japanese manufacturing changed since 1950?

b Suggest reasons for the change.

indicator not just of developmental progress, but also of the general well-being of society and its quality of life (see **Chapter 3 Section B**). In terms of international comparisons, it is more meaningful to compare Japan with other advanced economies, rather than with other countries in the Asian Pacific region (**2.3**).

Figure 2.3 Expenditure on social security, medical care and education

	Social security benefit (% GNP)	Medical care (% GNP)	Expenditure per school pupil (Y1000)
Japan	10.0	6.6	731
UK	6.2	6.1	497
France	17.7	8.6	582
Germany	10.8	7.4	551
USA	7.7	11.1	791

Review

6 Explain the link between economic prosperity and leisure.

7 What conclusions do you draw from the data in **2.3** about levels of social and welfare provision in Japan?

SECTION C

Explaining successful development – external factors

There are many less-developed countries (not just in the Asian Pacific region) that are keen to discover the secrets of Japan's developmental success. How might they learn and benefit from the Japanese experience? The problem here is that Japan's success may have been the product of a particular or even unique combination of factors and circumstances, perhaps never to be repeated for any other nation.

Figure 2.4 Factors boosting Japan's development

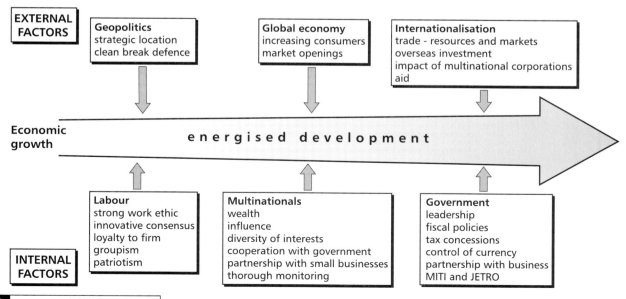

EXTERNAL FACTORS

Geopolitics
strategic location
clean break defence

Global economy
increasing consumers
market openings

Internationalisation
trade - resources and markets
overseas investment
impact of multinational corporations
aid

Economic growth

energised development

Labour
strong work ethic
innovative consensus
loyalty to firm
groupism
patriotism

Multinationals
wealth
influence
diversity of interests
cooperation with government
partnership with small businesses
thorough monitoring

Government
leadership
fiscal policies
tax concessions
control of currency
partnership with business
MITI and JETRO

INTERNAL FACTORS

In trying to answer the question raised at the beginning of the section, it may be helpful to identify two categories of contributory factor: the external (or international), and the internal (or domestic) (**2.4**). Please do not see them as being in two watertight compartments. In reality, they are often closely interwoven; there is interaction between them. Let us look first at the external or international dimension; the domestic factors are examined in **Chapter 3**.

The bonuses of war

Clearly, there were fortuitous events of a geopolitical nature that created opportunities (**2.4**). For example, the Korean War (1950–53) highlighted the strategic importance of Japan's offshore location with respect to the Asian continent. At that time, the mainland was being overrun by communism. The USA and its Western allies soon realised the need to keep down-and-out Japan as a member of the capitalist camp, rather than let it slip into the hands of the communists. So rather than continue punishing the defeated Japan for its part in the Second World War, help was given to rebuild its economy. Japan was able to regain face and become rehabilitated as a respected member of the global community. Another bonus was not being allowed to rearm; instead, Japan was able to shelter under the defensive umbrella provided by the USA. In short, since then Japan has never had to spend more than 1 per cent of its national wealth on defence.

Later, the prolonged war in Vietnam (1957–75) presented another opening. Whilst US industry was preoccupied with meeting the needs of the war effort, Japanese manufacturers were given the chance to produce and sell an increasing range of consumer goods for the affluent North American market.

Figure 2.5
Internationalisation of the Japanese economy

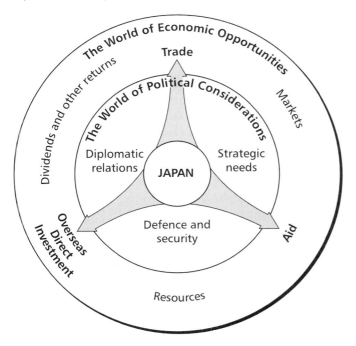

Before leaving the subject of war, it should be pointed out that defeat at the end of the Second World War presented Japan with an opportunity. Ironically, the profound destruction of its industrial infrastructure gave Japan, as it were, a clean slate on which to make a new industrial beginning.

Internationalisation

The Japanese economy has grown by spreading its tentacles to touch almost all parts of the world (**2.4** and **2.5**). Growth has been drawn in from offshore. In many respects, Japan has had no option. For example, because it lacks mineral and energy resources, it has had to obtain these basic material requirements of industrialisation from overseas. To be able to buy them, it has had to sell, principally manufactured goods. Fortunately, there has been an expanding market overseas for the goods Japan has produced. The home market for consumer goods also grew as the economy began to pick up. Inevitably, then, trade became one of the critical economic links to the outside world – tapping resources and accessing markets.

Review

8 With reference to **2.5**, explain and illustrate how each of the three economic links might be affected by political considerations.

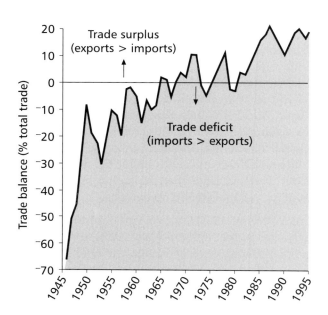

Figure 2.6 Japan's changing trade balance (1945–95)

Trade

One might be tempted to say that Japan has been too successful as a trading nation. Nowadays it has a huge overall trade surplus (**2.6**). A significant number of Japan's trading partners, including the USA and the UK, suffer large trade deficits. Complaints are made and threats of protectionism are uttered, thereby creating a tension referred to as **trade friction**. The interesting trend shown by **2.6** is how Japan's trade balance shifted from a massif deficit to a mammoth surplus. Curiously, the move into surplus coincided with the beginning of the low-growth era(**2.1**). The USA is by far the most important of Japan's trading partners. As a consequence, the trade flows between them may be seen as a strong sinew binding the eastern and western shores of the northern Pacific Rim.

It is Japan's post-war performance as an exporter that draws much attention and most fear or admiration. The view is that the whole growth of the Japanese economy has been 'export-led'. It is currently responsible for about 10 per cent of all the world's visible exports (the USA's share is 13 per cent, the UK's 5 per cent). Japan's export commodities have changed a lot since 1955 (**2.7**), following shifts in Japanese manufacturing. Textiles have declined, so too have metals like iron and steel. More than compensating for this has been the growth in machinery and equipment. This broad category now accounts for three-quarters of all exports. It includes such products as motor vehicles and ships, electrical and electronic goods. In other words, it includes many of those consumer goods for which Japan is famous throughout the world.

Nearly 40 per cent of Japan's exports go to Asia, particularly the Pacific Rim countries. North America is the next most important destination. The share of exports going to Western Europe has been increasing steadily. Just over 20 per cent of Japan's exports end up here, in particular the UK.

Figure 2.7 The changing composition of Japanese exports and imports (1955–95)

Exports (% of value)	1955	1965	1975	1985	1995
Foodstuffs	8	4	1	1	1
Textiles	40	16	5	4	2
Chemicals	5	7	6	4	6
Metals	15	17	18	11	6
Machinery & equipment	12	42	61	72	76
Others	20	14	9	8	9

Imports (% of value)	1955	1965	1975	1985	1995
Foodstuffs	25	1	13	12	17
Industrial raw materials	49	38	20	14	11
Mineral fuels	11	19	41	43	17
Machinery & equipment	13	26	21	17	22
Others	2	12	5	14	26

Japan is responsible for about 7 per cent of all the world's importing (so too the UK; the USA's share is 16 per cent). In terms of the commodity composition of Japan's imports, mineral fuels were dominant in the 1970s and early 1980s, when the two oil shocks greatly increased the price of crude oil (**2.7**). Since then, the world price of oil has fallen. Japan has also changed its energy strategy and is now using much less oil. So the percentage share of imports accounted for by mineral fuels has fallen dramatically. Foodstuffs now account for a similar share. Imported industrial raw materials have declined in importance. This reflects the change in Japanese manufacturing from heavy to light industries. It is interesting that Japan both imports as well as exports machinery and equipment. In fact, they account for 22 per cent of all imports, and represent the single largest category, most coming from the USA and Germany.

The geographic origins of Japanese imports are much the same as the export destinations. Asia, particularly the Rim countries, is the main source (45 per cent), followed by North America (25 per cent) and Western Europe (16 per cent).

Review

9 Try to answer each of the following questions.
 a Why has Japan's trade balance become favourable in the period of low growth (**2.6**)?
 b How are changes in Japanese manufacturing reflected in the changing composition of exports and imports (**2.7**)?

10 a What diagrammatic techniques might be used to illustrate the data in **2.7**?
 b Which technique do you think would be most effective?

11 The discussion in this section has been about **visible trade**. What is the difference between this and **invisible trade**?

12 What is the difference between the **balance of trade** and the **balance of payments**?

Overseas direct investment (ODI)

This is the second of the economic links responsible for the internationalisation of the Japanese economy (**2.5**). Overseas direct investment is about the ways businesses from one country become involved in the business life of another.

The ways include:

- setting up branch factories and branch offices, such as Sony have in various parts of the UK;
- agreeing joint ventures, such as that between Rover and Honda, and involving the exchange of technology, production methods or personnel management ideas;
- purchasing large amounts of equity (stocks and shares) in overseas businesses, thus allowing the investing company to influence what the foreign companies do.

Much of Japan's overseas investment has been made by its **multinational corporations**, namely huge conglomerates like Mitsubishi, Mitsui and Sony, with diverse business interests throughout the world. By 1995, investments amounting to nearly $500 billion had been made since 1951. The trend in new investment was generally upward until 1989, with three 'waves' of accelerated investment (**2.8**). A fourth possible wave may have been set in motion in the mid-1990s.

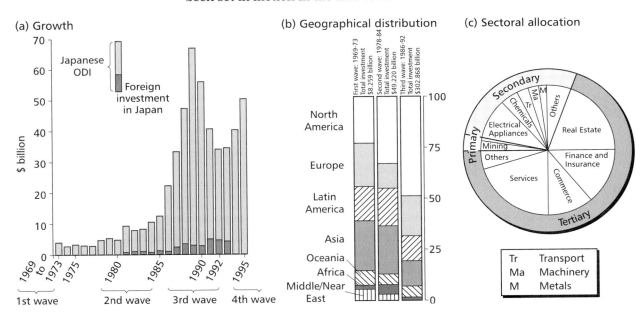

Figure 2.8 The growth and targeting of Japanese overseas investment

2.8 also analyses the geographical distribution of Japanese investment. During the 1960s and 1970s, half the investment went to developing countries in Asia and Latin America. In the third wave, however, something like 70 per cent of it was made in North America and Europe. The two leading recipients of Japanese overseas investment were the USA (42 per cent) and the UK (7.5 per cent). Why this apparent shift from developing to developed countries?

The shift is explained by a change in Japan's view of overseas opportunities. During the 1970s, overseas investment was about exploiting resources (particularly minerals, oil and gas) and using cheap labour in developing countries. Japan still needed raw materials for its scaled-down heavy industry. Japan needed to reduce its dependence on Middle Eastern oil. As labour costs rose, Japanese companies needed to move their factories to places where labour was cheaper.

In the 1980s Japanese firms saw new overseas opportunities. Two of them remain among today's main investment targets. They are:

■ the more advanced forms of manufacturing;
■ large financial institutions like banks and insurance companies.

These activities take place principally in the developed world. By setting up branch factories, Japanese firms are able to produce goods that can be substituted for direct exports from Japan (known as **export substitution**). This helps to reduce **trade friction**. Developed countries are also regarded as low-risk investment areas, by virtue of their political stability and the reliability of their financial institutions. However, there are already indications, at the beginning of what is being seen as a fourth wave of investment, of renewed Japanese interest in Asia. In 1995, although North America and Europe still accounted for 62 per cent of Japanese investment, Asia's share had risen to 24 per cent. Once again, much interest centres on Asia's huge reservoir of labour. Added to that, however, development in the Asian Pacific region is creating an expanding and increasingly affluent consumer market.

2.8 also looks at Japanese overseas investment in terms of economic sectors. There are some surprises. Mining – the working of minerals and energy – accounts for only 7 per cent of investment. More surprising is that only just over a quarter of ODI is backing manufacturing. Interestingly, the production of electrical goods takes a much larger share than motor vehicles. However, the outstanding feature of Japanese ODI today is that about two-thirds of it is supporting tertiary activities – finance and insurance, real estate, commerce and a diversity of services like tourism. As a result, much of Japanese ODI continues to end up in the developed rather than the developing world.

Like trade, overseas investment is a two-way thing. Whilst Japanese companies invest overseas, so overseas companies are investing in Japan. As with trade, the two flows are very uneven. Japanese outward investment is 16 times larger than total foreign investment in Japan. Over half of the latter is made by US companies; UK companies are responsible for less than 5 per cent. Eighty per cent of foreign investment in Japan is to do with manufacturing.

With both flows, countries of the developed world are the principal partners. In the case of North America, however, much of the investment may be seen as circulating within the Pacific Rim. By comparison, the countries of the Asian Pacific region are second-league players, but that may be beginning to change.

Review

13 With reference to 2.8:

a How has the value of overseas investment changed?

b How has the distribution of investment changed?

14 Apart from risk, can you identify any disadvantages for Japan resulting from its overseas investment?

Aid

It may seem a little odd to be including aid as the third of the links binding the Japanese economy to the outside world (**2.5**). The truth of the matter is that Japan has always adopted a rather pragmatic approach to aid and has never concealed its wish to put the act of giving to its own advantage. Much of Japan's aid has been directed towards SE Asian countries. For this reason, the whole matter will be examined in rather more detail in **Chapter 5**.

Finally, it should be stressed that internationalisation underlies another important feature of the whole development process: namely that no nation can afford to be an island. If countries are keen to develop to any significant degree, they have to interact on an international scale. The development cable needs to be energised from overseas (**2.4**). That interaction is going to be largely a matter of trade and direct investment, and both will be transacted on a two-way reciprocal basis. There can be no doubting that the large-scale offshore movement of the Japanese economy over the last two decades has helped to sustain the continuing development of the country. But at what costs back home?

Enquiry

1   Find out why Japan was a late-starter in terms of industrialisation.

2   Investigate how governments can protect their farmers from foreign competition.

3   Does the typical location of service activities in Japan differ from that in the UK?

4   'Three wars, three opportunities for Japan.' Explain what is meant by this statement.

5   a Make a list of all the major Japanese companies that you can think of.
    b Star those that have branches in the UK.
    c Classify them on the basis of the main type of business.

6   a Find out what is meant by export substitution and trade friction.
    b How and why might they be linked.

7   Why are overseas links so important in the explanation of Japan's successful development?

Japan: the leading economy

Explaining successful development – internal factors

Towards the end of the previous chapter, we looked at a number of external factors to explain Japan's economic miracle. Here, the explanation continues, but now in terms of contributory factors within Japan. We may recognise three as being particularly significant (**2.4**). They are not necessarily considered in order of importance.

Qualities of labour

Under this heading, it is certainly necessary to highlight a number of things that relate to what might be broadly called 'human resources'. With a population past the 150 million mark, Japan has plenty of labour. Not just that, but the labour supply has particular strengths, such as:

- a strong work ethnic and a healthy attitude to wealth;
- loyalty to the employer;
- well trained for the workplace;
- a willingness to embrace new work practices and new technology;
- a strong patriotism and keenness to help Japan regain face with the international community by peaceful economic means.

Review

1 Explain the signifi-cance of each of the listed qualities of labour.

Innovation in the workplace

Japan has pioneered important new ways of running businesses. These include:

- the 'just-in-time' production system in factories;
- decision-making by consultation between employers and employees;
- moving forward by consensus – no need for strong trade unions;
- close co-operation between the giant business conglomerates (Mitsui, Hitachi, etc.) and myriad small family businesses – strong sense of partnership in the national interest;
- close monitoring of the 'opposition' both at home and abroad;
- thorough market research, again both in Japan and overseas.

Figure 3.1 Japanese workers – a national asset

Review

2 Explain the significance of each of the workplace features itemised above to the success of Japanese businesses.

Review

3 a Suggest reasons why the Japanese government is so keen to promote the high-tech industries.

b Why is research and development (R & D) so important to high-tech industry?

Government intervention

Japan is often held up as a supreme example of the free-market economy. In fact this could not be further from the truth. Throughout the post-war period, Japan's economy has been carefully nurtured and managed by its government.

The intervention has taken various forms. For example, the government has maintained a strict control over the banks and as a result has been able to control exchange rates. It is claimed that such intervention has managed to maintain a slightly undervalued yen. This will have been to the benefit of exports, though not so good for imports. Tax policies have been quite effective in smoothing out the fluctuations in domestic demand that normally accompany the regular business cycle of boom and slump. Simply put, taxes are lowered during the slumps and raised during the boom periods. Other policies have encouraged private and corporate investment, particularly in manufacturing, while exporting has frequently benefited from tax concessions.

The arm of government responsible for much of this intervention is the Ministry of Trade and Industry (MITI). It is perhaps the most powerful and influential of all the ministries. Two further examples of its activities might be cited. The first has been its wish to achieve a more even distribution of manufacturing within Japan (see **Section B**). The so-called 'technopolis projects' are the most recent of a number of schemes with this aim in mind. These projects, one in each of the 48 prefectures, also demonstrate how the Japanese government has sought to shift the emphasis of manufacturing towards the cutting edge of the high-tech industries.

Possibly the greatest of MITI's achievements has been its monitoring of overseas markets and investment opportunities, as well as new technology. Working through a global network of economic intelligence gathering offices, known as the Japan External Trade Organisation (JETRO), MITI has conducted market research on a scale and with an efficiency unmatched by any other country. Once collected and analysed, the results of this monitoring are passed on to relevant businesses for appropriate action. This last point serves to underline the high level of co-operation between the public and private sectors. Indeed, it would be quite appropriate to refer to a working partnership between government and corporate business.

Multinational corporations

Much of Japan's economic power and wealth is in the hands of a small number of huge trading companies with considerable overseas business interests. The names of Japanese corporations like Sumitomo, Fuji, Matsushita, Mitsubishi and Mitsui are renowned throughout the world. Before the Second World War they were known as the *zaibatsu*, but today they are more commonly referred to as the *sogo shosha*. Most of them are active in, but by no means confined to, four economic areas: manufacturing, public utilities, banking and insurance, retailing and wholesaling. It is because of their immense resources and diversity of business interests that they have played such a vital part in Japan's economic success. The importance of that role has been increased by the high degree of cooperation between them and the government, and between them and hundreds of thousands of small, essentially family businesses.

Some handicaps

It would be wholly wrong to think that Japan's progress along the developmental path has not encountered any problems. In fact there have been some serious handicaps. Their existence perhaps serves to emphasise the importance of the positive factors already considered.

Besides lacking mineral and energy resources, the development process in Japan has been handicapped by the physical geography of the country. Only one-quarter of the land is suitable for development and settlement (**3.2**). Such land is in the form of small lowland areas, mainly coastal in

Figure 3.2 Densely settled fragmented lowlands

location, each separated from its neighbours by rather inaccessible upland. The creation of national transport networks has been a real challenge, made even more so by the island character of Japan. Linking the four main islands – Hokkaido, Honshu, Shikoku and Kyushu – by bridge and tunnel has involved major civil engineering projects. Above all else, though, usable land is a very scarce resource in Japan.

The costs of success

Not only have there been hurdles to overcome in advancing the development process, but the process has not always yielded benefits. Three significant costs are discussed here.

Unequal development

It is usual for economic growth and development to be concentrated at favoured locations. Such concentration gives rise to what are termed **cores** (see **E&P 30.3**). Japan is no exception here.

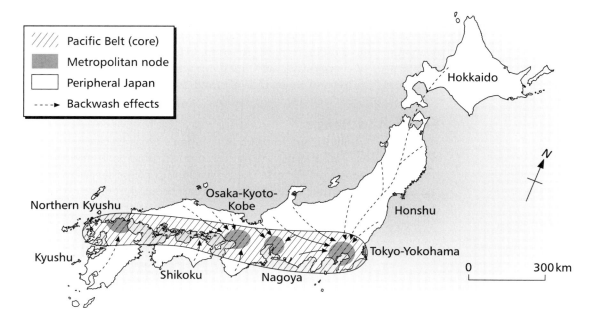

Figure 3.3
Japan's core and periphery

At the national level, Japan has a highly developed core in the form of the Pacific Belt (**3.3**). This is, in fact, linear in shape rather than round, stretching from Tokyo westwards to northern Kyushu. It embraces four distinct metropolitan nodes – Tokyo-Yokohama, Nagoya, Osaka-Kyoto-Kobe and northern Kyushu. The pattern of development in Japan has always shown this linear core. Up to the 17th century, it focused along the shores of the Inland Sea. Since then, it has gradually extended eastwards. The setting up of Edo (later renamed Tokyo) as a new capital city encouraged extension of the core in this direction. Today, the core's centre of gravity is very much at this eastern end.

You might ask: why does the core form in the first place, and what makes it persist and grow? These are not easy questions. A core develops when people exploit a particular resource, location or new technology. If they are the first, then what they have done is likely to stay ahead of the field. A process known as **cumulative causation** sets in. A momentum is created whereby the initial growth attracts more growth – success breeds success. This is an example of a **multiplier effect**.

Perhaps the most serious cost associated with the development of a core (a cost that is to the country as a whole) is that it grows at the expense of other regions. By what are known as **backwash effects**, it draws in resources, people and investment (**3.3**). The regions providing these things are known as the **periphery**. They lose whilst the core gains.

It is the loss of population that most hurts peripheral regions. It is usually the younger and more able people who leave. They are drawn to the core by its perceived attractions – a better job, higher wages, more services and so on. Once such people leave, there is a downward spiral of decline – a multiplier effect in reverse.

Economic activities suffer because of the loss of more enterprising workers. Losing them and their children affects population structure. It really means the loss of two generations. As the local population declines, so there are insufficient people left to support services like schools, hospitals and shops. As these services shut down, so the quality of life for the remaining people declines. This, in turn, can easily persuade even more people to move to the core.

Review

4 Compile a table listing the costs and benefits of core locations and peripheral locations.

The environment

There was dreadful pollution of air and water in Japan during the boom days of the late 1950s and 1960s. This was caused mainly by heavy industry. There was also immense habitat damage caused by the clearing of hill sides and the reclamation of wetlands to provide space for industrial sites and housing. At the time, no one really cared what was happening to the environment; economic success was the name of the game.

Slowly, the Japanese came to realise the damage to human health being caused by such pollution. It is now generally agreed that environmental scandals like 'Yokkaichi asthma' and 'Minimata disease' were turning points in Japanese attitudes towards the environment.

There is plenty of evidence to show that Japan has done much to clean up its environment since the 1960s. Today, it is responsible for 5 per cent of the world's carbon dioxide emissions. This compares with figures of 3 and 23 per cent for the UK and the USA. The amounts of sulphur dioxide and carbon monoxide in the air above Japan cities have fallen, but nitrogen dioxide continues to rise. Water pollution in rivers and along the coast, though still high, has dropped substantially.

Other vital steps include acceptance that environmental protection is a government responsibility. That responsibility is handled by the Environmental Agency. Thanks to Yokkaichi asthma and Minimata disease, it is also accepted that if a person's health is damaged by pollution, then the polluter must pay compensation – that is, provided a causal link is proved.

Japan is a much 'greener' society now than it was 30 years ago. All sorts of local initiatives are being taken to educate the public in such matters as recycling, litter and efficient resource use. Public participation in local initiatives to conserve and improve the environment is encouraged. Certainly, the quality of the Japanese environment has benefited. But some problems like noise, vibration, unsightliness and smell persist at unacceptable levels. Urban road traffic remains a serious polluter. Finding environmentally friendly ways of disposing of refuse, particularly plastics, is a major challenge. New worries centre on the safe disposal of harmful substances used by high-tech industries and the dangers of using too many herbicides and agricultural chemicals.

Quality of life

Whilst Japan as a nation has been highly successful, how have its ordinary people fared? How good is their quality of life? Let us focus on the latter question. First, we need to have some idea of what the term **quality of life** means. Literally, it means the degree of goodness in the living conditions and lifestyle of a person. So there are two main aspects: living conditions (housing, diet, services, safety, etc.) and lifestyle (leisure, affluence, work satisfaction, opportunities for personal advancement, etc.). There is not enough space to investigate all the components of quality of life. We will focus on just two, one from each of the two main headings: housing and leisure.

Housing

	Japan	UK	France	USA
Average floor space per dwelling (m²)	92.6	97.6	105.5	157.7
Dwelling floor space per resident (m²)	30.6	40.2	34	62.6
% of dwellings with underground sewerage	47	96	68	73
Spending on housing as a % of household budget	26	25	30	19
% of homes owned	60	68	54	64

	Tokyo	London	Paris	New York
Average price of residential land (Y1000 per m²)	560	30	29	10
Average house price (Y1000)	132	62	36	33
Cost of a detached house as a multiple of annual income (times)	12.9	6.9	3.4	2.9
Park area per resident (m²)	2.7	23	11.6	25.6

Figure 3.4 The housing situation – some international comparisons

Next to food and diet, housing is probably the most important aspect of living. Again, it is more appropriate to compare Japan with another advanced economy. The comparisons made in **3.4** suggest that Japan and its capital city do not compare very favourably. The clear message is that housing in Japan is small and expensive. This is particularly the case in Tokyo, where there is also relatively little space in the form of parks. All these unfavourable features are the outcome of Japan's overall shortage of usable land and the concentration of so much development in the core. However, it is quite clear from **3.5** that the Japanese home is well equipped.

	% of households
Colour TV	98.9
Video recorder	73.7
Washing machine	99.3
Refrigerator	97.9
Microwave oven	84.3
Air conditioning	74.2
Personal computer	15.6

Figure 3.5 Ownership of consumer durables

Leisure

Leisure is now the top priority in Japan when it comes to improving lifestyle (**3.6**). It has even overtaken housing as the area of greatest public concern.

Figure 3.6 Aspects of lifestyle the Japanese most want to improve

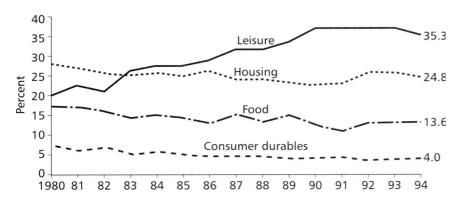

The average working week in Japan has fallen quite considerably and now compares favourably with that in other developed countries (**3.7**). Even so, although they are now entitled to more leisure-time than ten years ago, Japanese workers still only take just over half of their paid annual holiday. This perhaps confirms the workaholic image of the Japanese. At the same time, the survey may suggest that they are slowly realising that there is more to life than work, a secure job and material possessions.

Figure 3.7 The working-week in the factory (hours)

	Japan	UK	Germany	USA
1985	43.2	43.7	42.0	41.6
1995	39.3	43.1	39.5	42.6

The following conclusions might be made about the quality of life in Japan:

- development has undoubtedly brought an improvement in the Japanese quality of life;
- although Japan may be the world's second wealthiest economy, it is doubtful whether the country offers the second-best quality of life – certainly, key things like housing, leisure and welfare services are better in the UK;
- within the Asian Pacific region, it may be that some of the Tiger economies, notably Hong Kong and Singapore, are beginning to challenge Japan in terms of quality of life (see **Chapter 4**).

Review

5 Select six criteria that you think collectively make the best assessment of quality of life.

SECTION C

Current concerns about the future

There can be little doubt that the Japanese economy has passed its peak in terms of economic growth rates (**2.1**); for some 20 years it has been in a low-growth mode. Other countries in the Asian Pacific region, notably the Tigers, have been showing much higher rates of growth (see **Chapter 4**). But this is not to suggest that Japan is now on the path to economic decline and retrograde development. Far from it. Because of its internationalisation (**2.5**), it is unlikely that it will ever regress to any serious degree. Its web of global links provide a set of lifelines that would hold it up if it ever looked like going under.

Nonetheless, there are aspects of the economy that worry the Japanese. Cracks are beginning to appear. A number of these need to be highlighted.

The first is the issue of whether or not the expanding tertiary sector can produce the same sort of economic prosperity as has come from the growth of manufacturing (**2.1 and 2.2**). There is some unease that so much of the economy today is about providing services and recirculating capital, rather than producing jobs and creating new capital. That unease is intensified by the fact that productivity levels in the tertiary sector trail by as much as 50 per cent the levels currently sustained in North America and Western Europe.

Farming will continue to be an issue. The Japanese have always been highly emotive about farming. It is all to do with cultural attitudes, recent rural roots and the fear of running out of rice. Under international pressure, Japanese agriculture is becoming more exposed to market forces. The question is how much of it will survive?

The third worry is the internationalisation of the economy. Moving production overseas to cheaper labour and closer to resources and export markets makes good sense for Japanese companies, but what are the effects back home? Certainly, there are fewer jobs in manufacturing, but that is not necessarily a problem. The 'silvering' of the Japanese population is reducing the numbers of economically active people (**3.8**). Another likely outcome is that significant proportions of the profits from overseas activities will not return to Japan.

Figure 3.8 The changing age-sex structure of the Japanese population

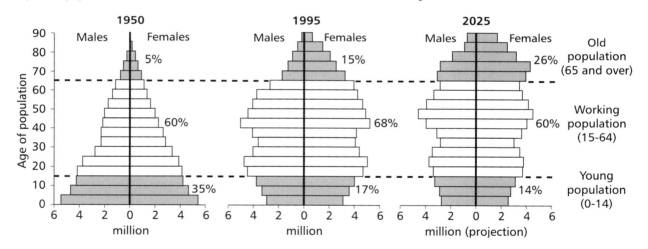

It is the offshore movement of manufacturing that sounds the loudest alarm bells in Japan. MITI is now openly warning that Japan's industrial base will become irreversibly 'hollowed out' if the present rate of offshore drift persists. The consequences are likely to be even more dire if the productivity of the service sector is not raised. At home, the Japanese government is keen to see the high-tech industries as its flagship. But such industries need very high levels of investment in technological research and development (R&D). At a time when the national budget is under great pressure and there is a tight squeeze on corporate funds, money for R&D is in short supply. To add to the worry, a recent survey showed that Japan lags behind the USA and Europe in key technologies – life sciences, new materials, oceanography, telecommunications and electronics.

In short, one can understand why the Japanese worry about their economic prospects in the 21st century and therefore their future quality of life. At the time of writing (1997), the recent collapse of some of Japan's leading banks and of its stock market has greatly added to that worry. Japan is approaching uncharted waters, but it is not alone. Can any country expect endless development and constantly rising living standards? Or does there come a time when a downturn must set in? At the moment, no one really knows.

Enquiry

1 **a** Identify ways in which the development gap between core and periphery may be reduced.
b In Japan's case, which of those ways seems most likely to produce the best results?

2 Write a report that identifies the main environmental costs of development in Japan.

3 Investigate one of Japan's multinational corporations.
a What are its main business activities?
b In which countries does it have branches?

4 Referring to **3.4**, **3.5**, **3.6** and **3.7**, how does the quality of life in Japan appear to compare with that in other developed countries?

5 Debate the statement that 'no nation can expect endless development.'

The four Tigers: Hong Kong, Singapore, South Korea and Taiwan

Introduction

Five states in the Asian Pacific region are classified by the World Bank as 'upper middle-income' economies – Brunei, Hong Kong, Singapore, South Korea and Taiwan. The last four (Brunei is somewhat different) are also often referred to as the 'newly industrialising countries' (NICs). Such a description was accurate enough 30 years ago. Today, however, these countries are well-established industrial producers, and a completely new generation of NICs has emerged . In the Asian Pacific Region today the up-and-coming economies include Indonesia, Malaysia, the Philippines and Thailand (see **Chapter 5**). The 'Asian Tigers' is another label given to Hong Kong, Singapore, South Korea and Taiwan. This seems altogether more appropriate, for what distinguishes them as a group has been their ferocious rates of economic growth. Although their economic take-off was less than ten years later than that of Japan, they have sustained high rates of growth over a longer period (**4.1**). Such has been their progress that they are now keen competitors of Japan, as for example in overseas trade. They seem to menace Japan rather like a tiger stalking its prey.

Figure 4.1 The Asian Tigers and Japan: some economic indicators

	Average annual rate of GNP per capita growth (1960–85) (%)	Average annual rate of GNP per capita growth (1985–95) (%)	Consumer price index (1995) (1980 = 100)	Trade per capita (1995) ($)
Hong Kong	7	4.8	327	45 761
Singapore	7.4	6.2	143	55 483
South Korea	6.6	7.6	242	3 767
Taiwan	9	7.2	180	7 713
Japan	6.1	2.9	131	4 849

	Arable %	Grass %	Forest %	Urban est. %	Roads (km per 1000km of land)	Railways (km per 1000km of land)
Hong Kong	6	1	22	65	802	35
Singapore	2	0	5	90	62	43
South Korea	19	1	65	10	16	31
Taiwan	24	11	52	10	543	108

Figure 4.2 Land use in the Asian Tigers

Figure 4.3 Sectors in the Asian Tiger economies

The umbrella term 'Asian Tigers' makes it tempting to think that we are dealing with four similar countries. However, **4.1** and **4.3** hint at some differences; **4.2** provides actual physical evidence.

	Agriculture		Industry		Services	
	% GDP	% Workers	% GDP	% Workers	% GDP	% Workers
Hong Kong	0	1	21	35	79	64
Singapore	0	0	36	35	64	65
South Korea	7	17	44	36	49	47
Taiwan	4	11	41	39	55	50

Review

1 Why do you think that these four countries are called 'Tigers'?

2 Referring to **4.1**, what comments would you make about changes in the rates of economic growth over the period 1960 to 1995?

3 What significance do you attach to the differences between the four countries shown by the data in **4.2**?

4 Highlight the differences between the four countries shown by the data in **4.3**.

The next four sections of this chapter look at each of the four Tigers in turn. From these, it is hoped to arrive at answers to two questions:

- Has development in these four countries followed a similar path?
- What are the reasons for the success of these economies?

Case studies

Case study: South Korea

Some of the statistics in **4.1** suggest that South Korea (officially known as the Republic of Korea) is not the strongest of the Asian Tigers. Yet it is the largest in area, population and economy (**1.5** and **1.6**). Perhaps the Korean War (1950–53) is partly to blame for its low ranking in per capita GNP. Widespread wartime damage and destruction, together with the earlier division of Korea into two states, could not have helped the development process. The border with North Korea today follows the cease-fire line of 1953. Technically, these two states are still at war, and that fact hangs as a cloud over the economic development of South Korea. Nearly 4 per cent of its GNP is spent on defence – another debilitating factor.

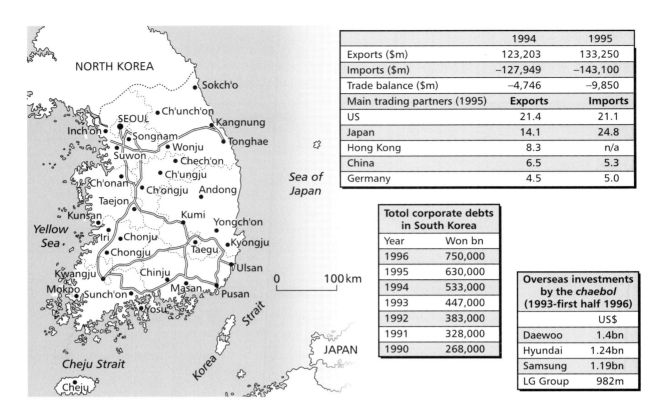

	1994	1995
Exports ($m)	123,203	133,250
Imports ($m)	−127,949	−143,100
Trade balance ($m)	−4,746	−9,850
Main trading partners (1995)	**Exports**	**Imports**
US	21.4	21.1
Japan	14.1	24.8
Hong Kong	8.3	n/a
China	6.5	5.3
Germany	4.5	5.0

Totol corporate debts in South Korea	
Year	Won bn
1996	750,000
1995	630,000
1994	533,000
1993	447,000
1992	383,000
1991	328,000
1990	268,000

Overseas investments by the *chaebol* (1993-first half 1996)	
	US$
Daewoo	1.4bn
Hyundai	1.24bn
Samsung	1.19bn
LG Group	982m

Figure 4.4 South Korea

Much of the economy of South Korea is in the hands of some 30 *chaebol* – giant business conglomerates, like the Japanese *sogo shosha*. Examples include Daewoo, Hyundai and Samsung (**4.4**). During the 1960s and 1970s there was a close partnership between these *chaebol* and the authoritarian government. The partnership played a vital part in the rapid industrialisation of the country. However, in the 1990s, public opinion has become rather anti-chaebol, principally because they are seen as corrupting politicians, aligning with military leaders and suppressing the growth of small businesses.

South Korea's early industrialisation was focused on heavy industries, which relied heavily on imported raw materials such as iron ore, coal and oil. As with Japan and the other Tigers, the character of manufacturing has since shifted towards the production of lighter goods, involving higher technology and mainly destined for the consumer market. Manufacturing generates a larger percentage of economic wealth in South Korean than in the other three Tigers (**4.3**).

Compared with the other Tigers, South Korea has a significant agricultural sector (**4.3**); this still accounts for 17 per cent of all employment. It has benefited from government protection in the form of import controls and heavy tariffs on imported food. This has certainly annoyed some of South Korea's trading partners, such as the USA.

Economists are agreed that the success of South Korea has much to do with the Korean people. Ethnically, the population is very homogenous. South Koreans are rated as being better educated, harder working and even tougher in business than the Japanese and Chinese. But in South Korea women are still regarded as second-class citizens; few of them reach the higher ranks of industry, finance and politics (**4.5**). Although wage levels generally are not as high as in the other Tigers, they have risen to the point where reforms in the labour market are being called for. Korean firms are beginning to look overseas for lower-cost locations. China is one such target, but the South Koreans are wary about transferring too much technology. They fear that once the Chinese have the technology, China will become a serious competitor in the world market. For the moment, South Korea is content to export to China such things as footwear and textiles, machinery and electronic goods in return for industrial raw materials and energy.

Figure 4.5 South Korea's labour problem

Ancient prejudices

The status of women in Korean employment and society remains woefully low **by Robert Taylor**

South Korea – more than most countries – is a male-dominated society. "It is going to take a long time to change the basic attitudes of men towards women," says Mih Yo Roh, vice-president of the Korean women's Development Institute, a state-run body committed to improving the status of women in society.

Mrs Roh says women are subject to sexual discrimination, forced to leave their jobs when they marry and have to retire earlier than their male counterparts. Women's wages average 55 per cent those of men and few women reach the higher ranks of industry, finance and politics.

The percentage of Korean women in the employed workforce was 48.3 last year, compared with 37 per cent 20 years ago. Most women are in low-paid jobs in manufacturing and services.

South Korea is not unique in its under-use of women at work. But disturbing trends provide evidence of more widespread oppression than elsewhere. Violence against women, especially abuse by husbands of wives, is growing.

Many in Korea blame Confucian values with its glorification of men over women for this. "It teaches that women's place is in the home and and women are an inferior species to men," says Mrs Roh.

Social change accompanying rapid urbanisation and the development of a more service-oriented labour market may help modify such prejudice. State backing for an end to gender discrimination may also help. A far more effective stimulus for change, however, may be South Korea's serious labour shortage as however resistant South Koreans are to employing women, their dislike of employing foreigners may prove stronger.

Economic hangover turning an Asian tiger into a tortoise

Oliver August on the problems sabotaging South Korea's boom

The South Korean economic miracle is blooming in Britain but wilting at home. The country is by far the biggest UK inward investor. Four of the top 20 foreign companies coming to Britain are from Korea with LG and Samsung, the industrial conglomerates, at number one and two on the list, having created tens of thousands of UK jobs in the 1990s.

The domestic Korean economy, however, is rapidly turning from an Asian tiger into a tortoise. Chinks in Korea's industrial armour have been exposed. The country's main problem is the inefficiency and low flexibility of its labour force. The labour issue will be the most critical factor in our

economy this year, said Sakong Eun-duk, senior economist at the Hanwha Economic Research Institute.

The problem is twofold. Salaries have been rising rapidly in recent years as workers demanded their share of the economic miracle. With the average wage equal to $10,000 they could afford few of the goods they were producing so well. The resulting rise in labour costs meant that building new production facilities in Korea became less attractive. Instead, the Koreans came to Britain. Last autumn Hyundai revealed plans for a £2.4 billion semi-conductor plant in Scotland.

The second aspect of Korea's labour force problem is inflexibility.

The Korean economy is dominated by a small number of conglomerates who offer their workers jobs for life. Competition between companies or employees is far from the norm.

To fight the industrial malaise, the Korean Government has now introduced new labour laws undoing decades of near total job security by allowing employers to lay off workers, hire temporary staff and replace strikers.

These changes have sparked nationwide protests. The streets of Seoul have been filled with 200,000 striking workers, who have called for the removal of the government over this issue, and violent clashes with the police seem inevitable.

In addition to solving the labour problem, it would seem that South Korea's prospects are closely tied to possible longer-term developments in the contracting communist world, namely:

- reunification with North Korea (see **Chapter 6 Section B**);
- creating economic links with the former Soviet Union and Eastern Europe;
- exploiting the complementarity that exists between the Korean economy and that of China.

Of all the Tigers, South Korea has been hardest hit by the recent slump in the fortunes of the Asian Pacific region. Althought it is hoped that the region will soon recover, South Korea has had to be bailed out by the International Monetary Fund. The crisis has brought into focus the need for governments, businesses and investors to behave more responsibly. Going for quick profits can easily lead to catastrophe.

Review

5 a What do the two percentage values shown in **4.3** tell you about farming in South Korea?

b How does South Korea compare with Japan in terms of agriculture's contribution to economic growth? (See **2.2**.)

6 Read the first newspaper cutting in **4.5**.
a Identify the changes in the South Korean economy that are likely to lead to greater sex equality.
b Give your reasons for arguing that sex equality is an important strand in development.

7 Read the second newspaper cutting in **4.5**.
a What aspects of the labour situation are highlighted?
b How do you explain the paradox that whilst South Korean men worry about job security, the country has a 'serious labour shortage'?

Case study: Taiwan

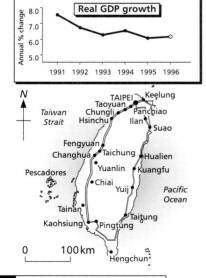

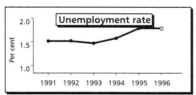

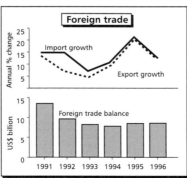

Taiwan (formally the Republic of China) occupies an island (formerly known as Formosa) (**4.6**). It is the second largest Asian Tiger (**1.6**) and came into being as a state during the Communist take-over of mainland China in the late 1940s. The overthrown Nationalist government and its supporters took up exile here and declared their independence from mainland China. They were subsequently followed by large

Figure 4.6 Taiwan and some recent indicators

numbers of immigrants. Like South Korea, Taiwan has had to live with the fear of being invaded. Nearly 6 per cent of its GNP is spent on defence.

The Taiwanese economy is heavily dependent on manufacturing (**4.3**). Roughly 40 per cent of GDP and employment is created by this sector. This is quite surprising, bearing in mind that Taiwan, like Japan, possesses few natural resources, apart from coal. It imports around 80 per cent of its energy. Similarly, Taiwan's early economic success was based on heavy industries like steel and shipbuilding, but more recently there has been a shift to industries that use relatively small amounts of raw material and make high value-added products such as electrical and electronic goods. There has also been a move to high-tech industries. Manufactured goods account for 85 per cent of Taiwan's exports.

Taiwanese industry shows a dual structure of many small family firms working alongside large state-owned enterprises. It is important to note the latter for, although Taiwan is classified as a capitalist country, its economy is still subject to considerable government intervention and direction. Indeed, the government has been quite authoritarian. Perhaps the most recent evidence of this direction is the continued concentration of industry in government-selected sites, such as the two export-processing zones of Taichung and Kaohsiung (**4.6**).

Taiwan has more of its land given over to agriculture than the other Tigers – just over one-third (**4.2**). The climate is good for growing a range of crops, from rice and vegetables to bananas and sugar cane. Mechanisation and agricultural research and development have allowed Taiwan to raise agricultural output, despite a marked fall in the agricultural labour force (now 11 per cent of total employed).

Although Taiwan's economic growth rate seems to be declining, its continued success can be attributed to a number of factors:
- a favourable trade balance created by effective exporting of competitively-priced goods;
- a government determined to prove itself, particularly to China;
- a ruthlessness in business;
- a strong inclination to take risks;
- a keen work ethic.

However, the future prospects of Taiwan are currently dulled by four things. First, there is its heavy reliance on trade, and its recurrent trade surpluses (**4.6**). Secondly, as in South Korea, the high wages expected by Taiwanese labour are already forcing firms to move offshore to lower cost areas such as the Philippines, Indonesia and Thailand. Thirdly, there is the strained relationship with China. China has made no secret of its wish for Taiwan to return to the fold. Equally, Taiwan has declared its preference for autonomy and the idea of 'one China, two governments'. Finally, like South Korea, Taiwan is currently suffering from the collapse of business confidence in the Asian Pacific region. The hope is that this is only a temporary blip.

Review

8 Write a brief account of the important trends shown by the graphs in **4.6**.

9 Which of the four factors mentioned in the last paragraph do you think is likely to have the greatest impact on Taiwan's future prospects? Justify your opinion.

Case study: Singapore

The Republic of Singapore came into being as a city state in 1959, when it ceased to be a British colony (**4.7**). This newly-won independence was given up in 1963 when Singapore joined the Malaysian Federation. But this political arrangement was to last only two years. Since 1965 Singapore has gone its own way, and very successfully so. From a situation of high unemployment, poverty and political unrest, Singapore has been transformed into one of the most affluent nations in the world. The rise is made all the more remarkable by the smallness of the island that is Singapore (**1.6**) and the fact that it has to import all of its water, most of its food and all of its energy and industrial raw materials.

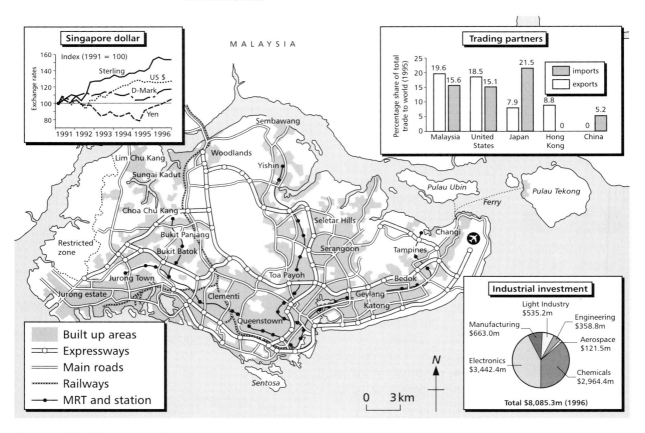

Figure 4.7 Singapore and some recent indicators

In response to clear government direction, the economic development of Singapore has gone through three stages:

- Up to the mid-1970s, export-oriented industry was encouraged, as well as foreign investment in Singapore by multinational companies. This proved highly successful.
- Industrial restructuring took place in the late 1970s involving a shift from labour- to capital-intensive industries. The result was much automation and considerable broadening of the product base.
- Since the mid-1980s, the emphasis in the economy has moved from manufacturing to services (**4.3**).

Figure 4.8 Singapore: a modern city state

Review

10 Explain the part played by location in Singapore's successful development.

11 What have been the costs and benefits of Singapore's firm government?

Singapore's remarkable success as a modern city state (**4.8**) would seem to be explained largely by three factors:

- Its natural harbour and the related port functions. Of all the Tigers, Singapore is the most dependent on overseas trade.
- The quality of human resources – 75 per cent Chinese, 15 per cent Malay, 5 per cent Indian – well-educated, hardworking and ambitious. The only problem here is a shortage of unskilled labour and professional people.
- The firm leadership provided by the Singapore government. However, this includes a tight control on behaviour, restricted freedom of the press and a largely one-party democracy.

Case study: Hong Kong

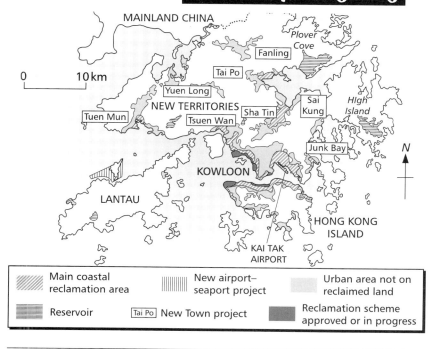

Like Singapore, Hong Kong was formerly a British Crown colony. It too is small in extent, covering an area of a little over 1000km². It comprises the island of Hong Kong, together with, on the mainland, Kowloon and the New Territories. Apart from its good harbour, it too lacks natural resources. With a density of around 5 500 persons per km², it is one of the most densely populated areas of the world (**1.6**).

Figure 4.9 Hong Kong – urbanisation and land reclamation

As with the other three Asian Tigers, there is a Chinese connection. In this case, it is particularly strong. The colony of Hong Kong was originally won in stages from the Chinese. First, in 1841 the island of Hong Kong was ceded to Britain (**4.9**). This was followed in 1860 by the acquisition of most of Kowloon. In 1898 another treaty leased to Britain for a period of 99 years the rest of Kowloon Peninsula, the immediate hinterland (the New Territories) and 230 small islands. It was this treaty that was ultimately to lead to the return of the whole colony to China.

Today, the population of Hong Kong is almost exclusively Chinese. Many refugees came here from the Province of Guangdong during the Communist take-over of China in the late 1940s and early 1950s. Further waves of refugees entered the territory at various times during the next two decades. It is these people who have played such a vital role in Hong Kong's success. This largely immigrant population has been driven by a desire to make money and to achieve personal security. In pursuit of these aims, they have shown a strong work ethic, great enterprise and a willingness to take quite high risks in business.

Hong Kong's development has always been closely linked to its port function. It is the world's largest container port, and just before its return to Chinese rule it was among the top 12 trading countries of the world. Much of its heavy manufacturing is port-related, as for example the steel, shipbuilding and chemicals industries. Important though these industries are, the manufacturing sector is in fact dominated by textiles and clothing, followed by the electronics industry, plastics and the production of a wide range of consumer goods. It is in these light industries that Hong Kong has shown its particular ability to produce goods cheaply and to respond quickly to changing fashion and demand.

A third vital sector of the Hong Kong economy is its financial services, the efficiency and reliability of which has played a major part in making this one of the financial and investment capitals of the world. The Hang Seng Index is one of the barometers of global finance. Tourism has also been a highly lucrative activity.

In order to make room for all this development, a considerable amount of land reclamation has had to be undertaken (**4.9**). The scale has been even greater than in Singapore.

The significance of Britain's role in Hong Kong's success should not be understated. British rule was essentially 'non-interventionist'. The policy was always one of encouraging free trade, through:

- freeport status;
- low taxes;
- few controls on the exchange of foreign currency;
- ensuring reliable financial and business services.

Basically, the British provided good governance, particularly in the second half of the 20th century. A respect for the rule of law, an elected legislature, a Bill of Rights and strong anti-corruption measures were among a number of things that helped create the right business climate in which enterprise and the free market economy could flourish.

Even before the return of Hong Kong to Chinese rule, there were signs of increasing economic integration with the mainland. However, an important feature of the changing relationship in both trade and investment is its two-way nature. This point is well illustrated in **4.10**. Remember this case study when you read **Chapter 7 Section C**.

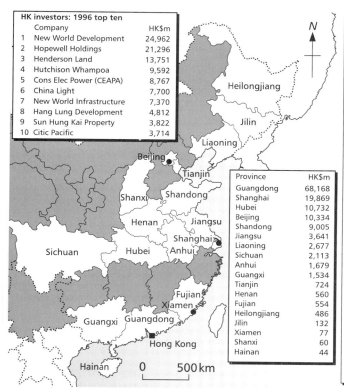

HK investors: 1996 top ten		
	Company	HK$m
1	New World Development	24,962
2	Hopewell Holdings	21,296
3	Henderson Land	13,751
4	Hutchison Whampoa	9,592
5	Cons Elec Power (CEAPA)	8,767
6	China Light	7,700
7	New World Infrastructure	7,370
8	Hang Lung Development	4,812
9	Sun Hung Kai Property	3,822
10	Citic Pacific	3,714

Province	HK$m
Guangdong	68,168
Shanghai	19,869
Hubei	10,732
Beijing	10,334
Shandong	9,005
Jiangsu	3,641
Liaoning	2,677
Sichuan	2,113
Anhui	1,679
Guangxi	1,534
Tianjin	724
Henan	560
Fujian	554
Heilongjiang	486
Jilin	132
Xiamen	77
Shanxi	60
Hainan	44

Six signs of tightening bonds with China

• China is Hong Kong's largest trading partner. In the first eight months of 1995, two-way trade rose by 18 per cent to HK$640bn. Eighty-eight per cent of goods re-exported through Hong Kong were destined for or originated from China.

• In the first eight months of 1995, 17.5m trips were made by Hong Kong residents to China, a 7 per cent increase. Hong Kong is China's most important source of external investment. By the end of June 1995, the cumulative value of direct investment from Hong Kong amounted to about US$68bn – around 60 per cent of total foreign investment.

• Much of Hong Kong's investment has been in Guangdong province. At the beginning of 1995, the cumulative value of Hong Kong's realised direct investment in the province was estimated at US$25bn, accounting for more than 70 per cent of the total. More than 16,000 companies involving Hong Kong interests were registered in Guangdong.

• China, along with the UK, is the largest outside investor in Hong Kong. At the end of 1994, total direct investment from China was estimated at about US$20bn.

• Financial transactions between Hong Kong and China have grown substantially. At the end of June 1995, external claims by Hong Kong's authorised institutions on China's banks and non banking entities reached HK$201bn and HK$65bn respectively. Their corresponding external liabilities to banks in China amounted to HK$237bn.

Figure 4.10 The growing bond between Hong Kong and China

With the expiry of the 99-year lease in 1997, Hong Kong is now once again part of China. Following the principle of 'one country, two systems', it has the status of a Special Administrative Region. The question that everyone is asking is what effect this return to China will have on Hong Kong – particularly the performance of its economy.

It is too early to say, but there are a number of pessimistic pointers. For example, the reputation of the current Government of China is hardly one of 'laissez-faire'. The prospect is one of more intervention and less freedom, be it of speech, political belief, movement or business decision-making. The Joint Declaration signed in 1984 by China and the UK concerning the return of Hong Kong stated that its rights and freedoms would be guaranteed for at least 50 years. The fact that China immediately replaced the agreed elected Assembly by one nominated by Beijing hardly augurs well for the future. However, China itself is currently moving away from hard-line Communism and that may eventually prove beneficial. For the moment, it seems most likely that if the business climate in Hong Kong does change, it will be in a way that dampens rather than nurtures the enterprise and economic growth that brought it to such prominence.

Review

12 Explain how and why 'good governance' was important to Hong Kong's emergence as a Tiger.

13 Read **4.10** and suggest a heading for each of the six bullet points.

Towards a model of economic growth

In these studies of the four Asian Tigers, and the earlier investigation of Japan, it is possible to see a number of recurring features in the economic growth that has powered development. Whether we can call **4.11** a model of economic growth is a matter for debate. Perhaps the acid test is whether those countries now in the earlier stages of development, to be considered in the next three chapters, also show similar features. Common sense suggests that circumstances in the first half of the 21st century may differ from those that prevailed in the second half of the 20th century. Consequently, the expectation may well be that the power behind development will also change, along with its outcomes.

Figure 4.11 Common features in the economic growth of Japan and the Tigers

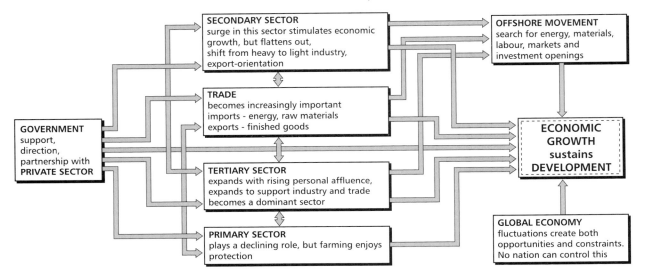

Explaining success – some key questions

So much for a possible development model, but are we able to tease out particular reasons for the rise of the four Asian Tigers? If we can, then how do the reasons compare with those previously identified in the case of Japan (**2.4**)? Is each of the five case histories unique, or do they show recurring features that we might isolate and build into some more general explanation of development?

Our search for an explanation of success is helped by attempting to answer three questions that arose originally in the case study of Japan.

Has timing been a factor?

Yes: as with Japan, it has been in two respects. First, the Tigers' development coincided with a period of spectacular growth in the global economy. Since the end of the Second World War (1945) there have been huge economic opportunities for the taking. Hong Kong and Singapore cashed in on the enormous boom in international trade, while all four produced the sorts of goods demanded by an expanding and increasingly affluent overseas market.

Japan also capitalised on the same opportunities, but rather earlier. This was to be to the advantage of the Tigers. In its post-war reconstruction, Japan had experimented with and pioneered new technologies in a whole range of industries. When the Tigers subsequently moved into the same lines of manufacturing, they were able to take advantage of the Japanese experience. Japan had done the research and development, leaving the Tigers free to move straight into effective and modern production.

Another benefit of this timing was reflected in the costs of labour. One inescapable feature of economic success is that it eventually raises the cost of labour. Since workers expect to share in success, so wages rise. Japan has always been ahead of the Tigers in terms of economic development and seizing opportunities. Consequently, its labour costs have always been higher. Higher labour costs ultimately mean higher production costs and less competitive pricing. Clearly, the Tigers have and will continue to enjoy a relative advantage here vis-à-vis Japan. However, the Tigers in their turn are already finding their prices being undercut by producers in those parts of the Asian Pacific region where labour costs are even lower.

In short, so far as Japan is concerned, it may be that it is not always best to be first in the field. Being second or third may score on a number of counts!

Have political factors played a part?

In addition to the openings created by the post-war growth of the global economy and international trade, the political climate has been quite influential. For much of the second half of the 20th century, East and SE Asia were threatened by the spread of communism from its heartlands in China and the former Soviet Union. The USA and its Western allies felt that it was important for those countries under threat to have strong market economies and stable governments. Like Japan, all four Tigers were located on the front line in this confrontation with communism. Thus for strategic reasons, their development was encouraged by various forms of foreign assistance, from help with defence to transfers of capital and know-how.

With the collapse of much of the communist world at the end of the 1980s, the political situation changed profoundly. No longer preoccupied with survival, the Tigers have been free to play to their economic strengths.

Have internal factors been significant?

Attention has been drawn in all five cases to the richness of the human resources. The presence of a labour force motivated by a strong work ethic and a will to succeed has been of immense importance. Its value has been further raised by the instinctive business skills and enterprise that mark so many of the decision-makers. One might point out that in three of the cases, the human resources of the Tigers are largely of Chinese extraction. But 1000 million of them have not – as yet – done as much for China itself! So maybe we need to look at other factors.

In the cases of Singapore and Hong Kong, one can certainly point to the value of their large natural harbours. These have encouraged the growth of the port function that has played a pivotal role in the development of both countries.

The constrained physical extent of all four Tigers is an interesting feature. Is it significant, or just coincidental? A tricky question, but maybe a case can be made for the former. For example, compactness should make for easy and efficient transport and communication. These attributes are likely to be conducive to development, involving a sense of cohesion, a common identity and efficient government. So, perhaps 'small is beautiful' even in the context of development!

Government in all four territories has been keen to encourage development, but in different ways. In the cases of Singapore, South Korea and Taiwan, government has led from the front – often authoritarian and unyielding. In contrast, the colonial government of Hong Kong has been much more in the background – helping discretely rather than coercing. But the governments of all the Tigers have been motivated by the wish to show that their economic systems are superior to those of the centrally planned or communist states. Propaganda has been a powerful stimulus.

The discussion has unravelled just some of the factors contributing to the Tigers' success. The explanation is far from complete. There is much that we still do not know or understand. However, this should not stop us from moving on to a fourth and final question.

The Tigers and Japan

The obvious question here is simply whether the Tigers pose a serious threat to Japan. In suggesting that 'no' is the answer, it is accepted that Tiger competition initially persuaded Japan to begin moving manufacturing offshore. That offshore move was motivated by the need to find cheaper labour. But the Tigers are on the same upward spiral of labour costs and they, in turn, are beginning to move production offshore. On the other hand, it can also be argued that competition from the Tigers has been good for Japan. It has stopped Japan from becoming complacent – the Tigers snapping at Japan's heels have kept it on its toes.

Although the Tiger economies continue to grow at a faster rate than Japan, the threat is not as great as it might seem. None of the economies begins to approach Japan's in size and clout (**1.5**) – the largest Tiger economy, that of South Korea, is only one-tenth that of Japan's. What seems clear is that the Tigers, like Japan, will find that the spiral of economic growth eventually begins to flatten out; indeed, there are signs of this already happening. In South Korea there are high levels of corporate debt and labour unrest (**4.4** and **4.5**), while other indications include rising unemployment in Taiwan (**4.6**), the devaluation of currencies and stock market turmoil in the region, and uncertainty surrounding Hong Kong's new masters.

Looking to the future, one wonders what scope there might be for the relationship between Japan and the Tigers to become less competitive and more cooperative. This could prove beneficial to development on both sides.

Case study: Brunei

As a postscript to this chapter, something needs to be said about the fifth Asian Pacific country classified, along with the Tigers, as higher middle-income (**1.5**). Up until 1984 this tiny country was a British protectorate (**1.6**). Its relatively high per capita GNP figure is easily explained: Brunei possesses huge reserves of oil and natural gas; these two commodities account for over 90 per cent of exports.

The revenues derived from the sale of oil and natural gas have been utilised for the benefit of the small population. There is free medical treatment, education and pensions; the costs of food and housing are low thanks to government subsidies. The interest in Brunei lies in the fact that, whilst the people enjoy a high standard of living, there has been little development as such. Other than providing the services just mentioned, one can point only to the construction of an international airport, a deep-water port and roads. Recently, there have been some moves to encourage agriculture, and thereby reduce the level of dependence (currently 80 per cent) on imported food. Brunei's small population must mean that the scope for industrialisation is very limited. So, in terms of its development path, Brunei is very much the exception to any rules that may have been established so far in this book. Adding to that uniqueness is its combination of 'democratic' government and absolute rule by the Sultan of Brunei.

Review

14 Identify the ways in which Brunei's development path differs from that of the four Tigers.

Enquiry

1   What is meant by the consumer price index (**4.1**)? Why is it important in the study of economic development?

2   Find out what has happened to the South Korean economy since 1995.

3   Find out what has happened to Taiwan's economy since 1995.

4   Imagine you are an industrialist setting up a new factory making electrical goods. Which one of the three export-processing zones (Taichung, Kaosiung or Nantze) would you choose for your factory (**4.6**)? Give reasons.

5   Find out what has happened to the Singapore economy since 1995.

6   Find out how Hong Kong has fared since its return to Chinese rule in 1997. Are you surprised by what you have found out?

7   Find out about Brunei's physical environment. What crops do those physical conditions most favour?

8   Which one of the factors – timing, human resources and government intervention - do you think has been most important in explaining the Asian Tigers' success?

9   'Japan and the Tigers have followed the same development pathway.' To what extent do you agree with this view?

10 How far does the explanation of the Tigers' success differ from that of Japan's success? (Reread **Chapters 2 Section C and 3 Section A.**)

11 Suggest ways in which Japan and the Tigers might cooperate. Would there be equal benefits?

Dependence or interdependence?

Indonesia, Malaysia, the Philippines and Thailand

SECTION A

Introduction

In this chapter, there is more emphasis on the international dimension of development. From what has been covered so far, it should be clear that a key aspect of national development is its wider international context (**2.5 and 4.11**). The examples drawn from the Asian Pacific region clearly demonstrate this; the implication is that development proceeds at a snail's pace, if at all, when a country is isolated from the mainstream of global life (see **Chapter 6**). The international links of trade and investment are crucial. So too is aid – not just for the poor receiver nations, but also for the donors. Whilst most of these links are promoted or sanctioned by governments, private sector organisations such as multinational companies also are frequently powerful and influential players in the whole development business.

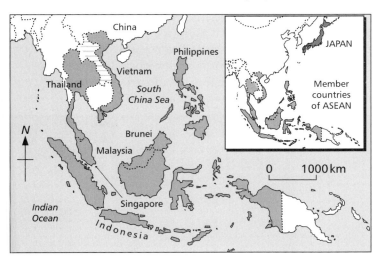

Figure 5.1 The member states of ASEAN

The international links that feed development extend across the scheme of four economic groupings that has been adopted in this book. For example, Japan's rise to become a high-income economy has been driven by trade, investment and aid contacts with both upper middle-income and lower middle-income economies. Those economies have also drawn development from the same links. Thus we might begin to see the whole development process as involving a complex set of international relationships. The following key questions then arise:

- Do these links or relationships bring mutual benefits to both parties? Do they create an equal partnership and a state of affairs that we will term **interdependence**?
- Or are the benefits rather one-sided? Do they create what we will term **dependence**, in which the weaker partner is subservient to, and exploited by, the stronger?

We will try to find answers to these question by investigating the links that exist between Japan and four of a grouping of seven Asian Pacific region countries, collectively known as the Association of South East Asian Nations (ASEAN) (**5.1**).

Case study: ASEAN

Review

1 Define **dependence** and **interdependence**, and illustrate the difference between them.

2 Referring to 1.5, work out what proportion of the economic wealth of ASEAN comes from the four lower middle-income economies.

ASEAN was established in 1967 at a time of great instability in the region caused largely by the gradual withdrawal of European colonial rule and the spread of communism. Besides striving for regional peace and political stability, the objectives of ASEAN include accelerating economic growth, social progress and cultural development, and providing mutual assistance in education and technical training.

The founder members were Indonesia, Malaysia, the Philippines, Singapore and Thailand. In 1984 they were joined by the newly-independent Brunei and in 1995 by Vietnam (**5.1**). Clearly, ASEAN embraces a diversity of countries at different stages of development. The membership in fact includes representatives of three different economic groupings – higher middle-income (Brunei and Singapore), lower middle-income (Indonesia, Malaysia, the Philippines and Thailand) and low-income (Vietnam). Thus a look at ASEAN and its links with Japan allows us to put the spotlight on one of those groupings – the lower middle-income economies.

SECTION B

The four lower middle-income economies

Although these countries fall within the same economic grouping, the per capita GNP data given in **1.5** suggest that there are differences between them. Some economists also refer to them as the 'recently-industrialising countries' (RICs) – second generation NICs, as it were, following in the footsteps of the Asian Tigers. It is the degree of industrialisation that largely accounts for the differences in per capita GNP.

Figure 5.2 Economic sectors of the lower middle-income economies

	Agriculture		Industry		Services	
	% GDP	% Workers	% GDP	% Workers	% GDP	% Workers
Indonesia	19	56	40	14	41	30
Malaysia	19	26	35	28	46	46
Philippines	22	45	33	16	45	39
Thailand	10	67	39	11	51	22

	Arable %	Grass %	Forest %	Urban est. %	Roads (km per 1000km² of land)	Railways (km per 1000km² of land)
Indonesia	9	7	60	15	157	4
Malaysia	3	0	59	25	59	5
Philippines	19	4	34	25	75	4
Thailand	33	2	26	15	70	8

Figure 5.3 Land use in the lower middle-income countries

Case study: Indonesia

Review

3 With reference to **5.4**:
   a identify the types of manufacturing being backed by foreign investment;
   b what other parts of the Indonesian economy appear to interest foreign investors?
4 Explain how each of the four bullet points above acts as a brake on development.

The Republic of Indonesia is by far the biggest of the four lower middle-income countries, in both area and population **(1.6)**. Indonesia comprises some 13 500 islands, half of which are inhabited. Sumatra, Celebes and Java are easily the largest of the islands belonging exclusively to Indonesia, but the country also accounts for three-quarters of Borneo and half of New Guinea **(5.1)**. It has a good resource base which includes large stocks of timber, oil and natural gas, tin and nickel.

The large population is remarkably homogenous, being mainly of Malay and Papuan origin. The Indonesians remain a predominantly rural people, with farming occupying over half the workers **(5.2)**. Only one-third of the population lives in a town or city **(1.6)**. Two-thirds of the people live on Java (one of the most densely populated islands in the world). This concentration of people aside, there are several other reasons why this island is the Indonesian core:

- it contains the capital city, Jakarta (pop. 10 million);
- it is a major producer of oil and minerals;
- its production of rubber, coffee, cocoa, sugar and cinchona bark are important exports.

At present, Indonesia is probably the least developed of the four RICs **(1.5)**. Over one-third of its exports are made up of primary products – oil and gas, rubber and sugar, timber and metal ores. Manufacturing accounts for 40 per cent of GDP, but employs only 14 per cent of the workforce **(5.2)**. Much of it is under the control of foreign companies **(5.4)**. Manufacturing mainly takes the form of branch plants set up to take advantage of cheap land and labour, as well as ready access to raw material sources.

There appear to be a number of impediments to Indonesia's development:

- the persistence of a military-backed government and the virtual absence of political freedom;
- territorial disputes in Timor and Irian Jaya;
- the prevalence of corruption, waste and poverty;
- the keenness of the powerful wealthy elite to maintain the status quo.

Indonesia has the requisite resources for substantial development advancement. However, it seems likely that only a revolution can remove the human barriers to development.

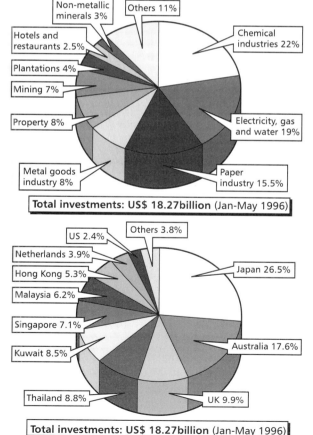

Total investments: US$ 18.27billion (Jan-May 1996)

Non-metallic minerals 3%
Others 11%
Hotels and restaurants 2.5%
Chemical industries 22%
Plantations 4%
Mining 7%
Property 8%
Electricity, gas and water 19%
Metal goods industry 8%
Paper industry 15.5%

US 2.4%
Others 3.8%
Netherlands 3.9%
Hong Kong 5.3%
Japan 26.5%
Malaysia 6.2%
Singapore 7.1%
Kuwait 8.5%
Australia 17.6%
Thailand 8.8%
UK 9.9%

Total investments: US$ 18.27billion (Jan-May 1996)

Figure 5.4 Foreign investment in Indonesia, by sector and country of origin (1996)

Case study: Malaysia

The Federation of Malaysia is made up of three components – peninsular Malaysia, and the states of Sarawak and Sabah on the island of Borneo. Up until 1957 Malaysia was a British colony. In 1963 the Federation was joined by Singapore, but only for two years. Compared with Indonesia, Malaysia is something of a midget (1.6).

Although the physical environment may be characterised as forested mountain with a hot humid climate, like Indonesia it is rich in natural resources (5.3). Besides tropical hardwoods, there is much potential energy in the form of oil and natural gas, together with metal ores such as tin, iron, bauxite and copper. Relative to its population and area, Malaysia is arguably the best endowed of the four nations in this grouping. Indeed, it has one of the best resource bases in the whole of the Asian Pacific region.

Few would doubt that Malaysia's development prospects look very bright. Given its resources, good physical infrastructure, stable government and sound economic policies, one might wonder why it is only now that Malaysia is taking off. Why was Malaysia not one of the original Asian Tigers?

Part of the answer may lie in the fact that until relatively recently, much of the economy was concerned with the production and export of raw commodities – palm oil, rubber, timber, oil, natural gas and tin. For example, Malaysia still accounts for half the world's output of palm oil and a fifth of all natural rubber and tin. It was only in the early 1980s that Malaysia really began to develop export-oriented industries (like steel, cars and cement) that processed some of its raw materials. To these have since been added a range of light industries making both consumer and high-tech products.

Another part of the explanation is historical, in that Malaysia had to fight for its independence from the UK. This caused destruction and hampered development. Then for some time after independence, British companies continued to own a large part of Malaysia's economic wealth. Even today, only 75 per cent of that wealth is Malaysian-owned; the Japanese are among the other stakeholders.

Review

5 Which of the three factors discussed above do you think has been the most serious brake on development?

The composition of the Malaysian population provides a third element in the explanation. There are two significant minority groups: the Chinese (31 per cent of the population) and the Indians (9 per cent). There has long been tension between the Malays and the Chinese, mainly because the Chinese control much of the commercial life of the country. The Malays are suspicious that the allegiance of the Chinese is to China or Taiwan, rather than to Malaysia. However, legislation has now been passed which tries to steer a delicate path between achieving a better share of the country's economic wealth for the Malays and not alienating the Chinese community, with its enterprise and expertise.

Case study: The Philippines

Two geographical features of the Philippines present problems, so far as the country's development is concerned. The first is that the country occupies an archipelago of some 7 000 islands. The resulting difficulties of transport and communication make unity and cohesion hard to achieve (5.3). Secondly, there is the ethnic diversity of its 69 million people. The majority are of Malay stock, but there are also Chinese, Indonesian, Moros and Negritos elements. Over 60 per cent are Catholic (a consequence of 300 years of Spanish colonial rule); the rest are either Muslim or Buddhist. Between 1898 and 1946 the USA was responsible for government, but today the country is a democratic republic. For some 15 years, the country suffered at the hands of the repressive regime of President Marcos. Although this ended in 1986, a continuing destabilising factor has been the presence of communist insurgents.

Bearing these characteristics in mind, it is perhaps not surprising to find the Philippines somewhat lagging in development terms. It is still very much an agricultural country (5.2). Exports of primary products (timber, minerals and agricultural products) still account for 25 per cent of GDP and export earnings. Machinery and equipment figure prominently in both trade directions. By the standards of the region, the population is well educated. Sadly, this asset and the country's richness in natural resources have yet to be exploited in a way that generates significant development. One obvious direction is to encourage multinational companies to capitalise more on this cheap labour pool. Another is to set up export-oriented industries that process local raw materials.

Review

6 Assess the relative merits of the two possible ways forward in the development of the Philippines.

Case study: Thailand

The economic indicators in **1.5** suggest that the Kingdom of Thailand ranks next to Malaysia in terms of current level of development. However, whilst roughly two-thirds of the Thai working population are farmers, agriculture generates only 10 per cent of the country's GDP (5.2). The main agricultural region is the huge lowland that occupies the centre of the country. The monsoonal climate makes it and the much smaller lowlands of the Malay Peninsula, important centres of rice-production.

The main natural resources of Thailand are timber and tin; these figure quite prominently in exports, as do rice and rubber (5.5). Japan is the major destination of Thai exports, although its share has declined slightly during the 1990s.

Early manufacturing in Thailand was principally textiles (mainly silk) and footwear. These industries are now declining, in relative terms, as the Thai government offers strong incentives to foreign companies to set up factories along the Eastern Seaboard (the coastal zone to the south and east of Bangkok, the capital city). Two new ports have been built (Map Ta Phut and Laem Chabang), linked by road and rail to Bangkok. By the end of the

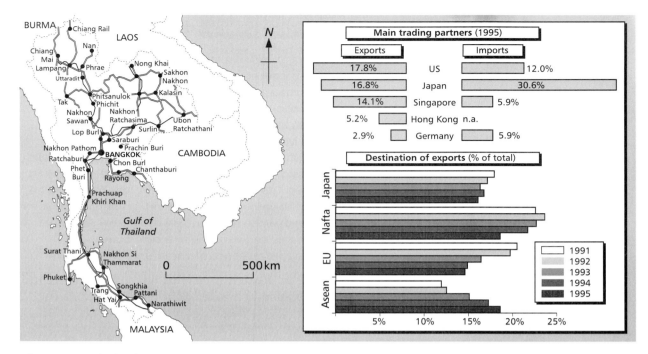

Figure 5.5 Thailand and its trade (1995)

Review

7 What conclusions do you draw from the big difference in the two percentage values shown for:
a Thai agriculture;
b Thai industry **(5.2)**?

8 Apart from their GNP per capita values, do the four countries have anything else in common?

century, this region is set to surpass Singapore in oil-refining and petrochemical output and to rival South Korea in steel-making. It is also expected to become Asia's largest centre for the manufacture of motor vehicles and vehicle parts outside Japan. High-tech industry is also being encouraged. At present, a shortage of labour in the region is causing wages to rise steeply, but population is expected to double within 15 years – a combination of inward migration and a high birth-rate. Clearly, we have a major core in the making. This growth may be impressive; but remember that cores have their costs.

Another noteworthy feature of the Thai economy is the relative importance of its service sector, which generates half the country's GDP **(5.2)**. A significant contributor here is the tourist industry. Over 5 million overseas tourists visited Thailand in 1996; two-thirds came from East Asia and nearly a quarter from Europe. The appeal of the country lies in its cultural and architectural heritage, its relatively cheap but modern hotels, its coast and, it has to be said, its tacky sex industry. It seems strange that tourism is much less developed in the other three countries, even though they command most, if not all of the resources just mentioned.

Up until the middle of 1997, all seemed to be going well with Thai development, but then there was a sudden loss of confidence in the Thai currency and stock market. Both plunged in value. This sent shock waves through the economies of the other three countries, as well as Singapore. It is impossible to tell at present whether this is just a blip or the beginning of a slowing down in economic growth and development within ASEAN.

The character of development

What, if anything, can we deduce from these four case studies concerning the character of development in the lower middle-income economies? The following seem to be recurring features:

- The primary sector, particularly agriculture, plays a more important part in generating economic growth (around 20 per cent) than has been the case in Japan or the Four Tigers (**2.2, 4.3** and **5.2**).
- Agriculture is very labour-intensive; in some instances it occupies more than half the labour force.
- Figures for manufacturing of around 35 per cent of GDP (not much less than in Japan and the Tigers) might suggest that this sector is well developed (**2.2, 4.3** and **5.2**). However, the relative importance of the industrial sector is perhaps exaggerated by the low productivity of agriculture and the modest state of the service sector.
- All countries are keen to industrialise. This ambition is being fulfilled by the growth of (i) industries processing primary products and (ii) branch plants set up by foreign companies keen to exploit low-cost locations (particularly cheap labour).
- As for trade, exports are largely made up of primary commodities, while imports are dominated by manufactured goods.
- In all countries the service sector generates most GDP – but only just (**2.2, 4.3** and **5.2**). The expectation is that the sector will gather momentum as the economies expand. The potential for tourism is considerable, but to date only Thailand has made use of it to an appreciable degree.
- All four countries have strong economic links with more developed economies, particularly Japan – a point explored in the next section.

Review

9 Critically discuss the above summary. Do you agree with the generalisations? Has anything been omitted?

The Japanese connection

The investigation of Japan's links with ASEAN will focus on the four lower middle-income countries.

Trade

Only Indonesia enjoys a favourable balance in its trade with Japan (**5.6**). As for the other three, if their trade deficits are expressed as percentages of the total value of trade (exports plus imports) the seriousness of their trading situation is brought into better focus. The deficit is particularly large in the case of the Philippines. As for the composition of this trade, exports to Japan are made up mainly of primary commodities and parts for assembly into finished goods. Imports are dominated by capital and consumer goods.

	Exports to Japan ($ million)	Imports from Japan ($ million)	Trade balance ($ million)	($ million)
Indonesia	12 917	7 672	+ 5 245	25.5
Malaysia	8 226	12 359	– 4 133	20.1
Philippines	2 652	5 892	– 3 240	37.9
Thailand	8 183	14 701	– 6 518	28.5

Figure 5.6 Trade with Japan (1994)

Review

10 On a global scale, which has attracted more Japanese investment – low-cost locations or markets? Try to explain why.

Overseas investment

The outstanding feature of Japanese overseas investment today is that over half of it is made in North America and Europe. About 25 per cent of that investment is to do with manufacturing; most of the remainder goes to finance and insurance, real estate and commerce. Less than 15 per cent of Japanese investment ends up in Asia; the ASEAN share is less than 8 per cent. The pattern of allocation is rather different, with more emphasis on manufacturing and primary activities (notably forestry and mining). Investment has two main aims, namely:

- to tap sources of timber, minerals and energy;
- to use cheap foreign labour in the manufacture of a range of finished and semi-finished goods.

In contrast with Europe and North America, the setting up of branch factories has not been driven by the wish to produce goods close to major markets. Levels of consumer spending in Indonesia, Malaysia, the Philippines and Thailand are still much lower than in the West.

Aid

In 1995 Japan accounted for just over half of all the aid being extended to countries in the Asian Pacific region. Well over half of this Japanese bilateral aid ended up in five ASEAN countries. Figure **5.6** monitors changes in that aid over four decades in terms of its composition and allocation to member countries. As regards the first, it is clear that as the relative importance of grant aid has fallen, so loan aid has increased; technical assistance has shown a steady rise. In short, the emphasis has shifted from straight giving, to aid that has to be repaid with interest.

Although ASEAN is a collective organisation, Japanese aid to the ASEAN countries has been allocated to countries on an individual basis; **5.7** shows that the allocation is very uneven. Indonesia

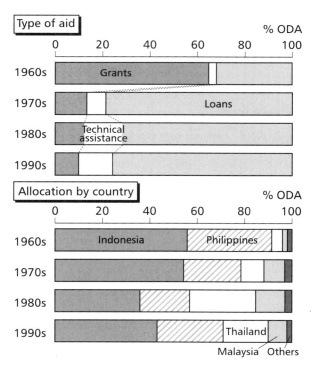

Figure 5.7 Japanese bilateral aid to ASEAN

(9 per cent of all Japanese aid) remains the single largest recipient within ASEAN, although its overall share has declined; so too has that of the Philippines (6 per cent) and Malaysia (1 per cent). As these three countries have faded, so Thailand has increased its share (4 per cent). The expectation is that Vietnam, the latest country to join ASEAN, will begin to receive considerable help from Japan (see **Chapter 6 Section B**).

Looking at the sorts of activities and projects that have been supported by Japanese aid in Indonesia and the Philippines, many are broadly related to the exploitation of natural resources. Electricity generation, road building, port development, airport modernisation and communications network schemes have been conspicuous. Loan aid provides the main support for such infrastructural projects, which account for roughly half of all Japanese aid. Whilst these projects undoubtedly help stimulate development, they do at the same time help investments being made in those countries by Japanese businesses. For example, a Japanese steel-maker keen to open up new supplies of iron ore will certainly be helped by the sorts of transport projects being supported by Japanese aid. In contrast, grants rather than loans back the more humanitarian and welfare-oriented undertakings, like irrigation and flood control projects, the building of hospitals and schools and the setting up of technical training schemes. It is this type of scheme that promises some benefits for poorer people rather than powerful companies.

Given Malaysia's long-standing ambition to become one of Asia's Tigers, it is hardly surprising that Japanese aid has been targeted mainly at creating the infrastructure and services necessary for industrialisation, from power generation to the opening of research establishments, from port schemes to advanced skills training centres. The declining amount of Japanese aid going in Malaysia's direction is confirmation that industrialisation has really taken off.

In Thailand, Japanese aid appears to be geared more to rural areas and to farming. Village electrification, irrigation and fertiliser production are three such activities being backed, along with a marked emphasis on education and training. This emphasis may be expected to raise the skills levels of the cheap labour being exploited by Japanese branch plants.

It is easy to be critical of the Japanese aid programme with its emphasis on loans, on the economic aspects of development and on securing material benefits for Japan. The Japanese have never concealed their highly pragmatic and rather selfish approach to aid. In the short-term, such aid inevitably creates a situation of dependence (on Japan) and exploitation. However, the Japanese view is that its aid programmes eventually encourage trade and investment as part of the development process. As these links grow, so the situation may change to become one of interdependence and mutual benefit. It also has to be said that the ASEAN countries are not averse to the general direction of Japanese aid. They too see the longer-term benefits. However, they do complain that there should be a greater transfer of technology and that their agricultural products should be given an easier access to the Japanese market.

Review

11 With reference to 5.7, identify how the allocation of Japanese bilateral aid changed between the 1980s and the 1990s. Suggest reasons for the changes.

The role of multinational corporations

Our analysis in **Chapters 2** and **3** showed that government guidance and intervention have been important factors in Japan's successful development. But a government can only do so much when it comes to overseas activities. If it does too much it can easily be accused of meddling in the affairs of another state. For this reason, much is left to be undertaken by the private sector and in Japan's case by its multinational corporations like Hitachi, Mitsubishi and Sumitomo. It is the wide diversity of their business interests, from mining right through to services, that makes these giant corporations so influential, particularly in trade and overseas investment. To a lesser extent, they contribute to Japan's bilateral aid programmes with technical assistance.

Japan's multinational corporations are the main instruments of the country's overseas search for resources and markets. The resources they tap range from timber to low-priced labour, from energy to cheap land. The markets they seek are not just for manufactured goods, but also for a variety of financial services. They are even in the business of opening up new tourist destinations for Japanese holidaymakers.

Case study: Sony

The following newspaper extract is about the Japanese giant Sony and its joint ventures throughout SE Asia and not just in ASEAN countries (5.8). Of the Japanese multinationals, the efforts of Sony are perhaps more focused on manufacturing than most.

Figure 5.8 Sony in Asia

	Facility	Start	Products
1	Taiwan Toyo Radio	1967	Radios, Walkmans, telephones, tape recorders
2	Sony Electronics of Korea	1973	Precision comp, CD Boomboxes, headphones, TV tuners
3	Toyo Audio	1984	Radios, Walkmans, telephones
4	Sony Video Taiwan	1984	1/2" VCR, multi-disc players
5	Sony Precision Eng. Center	1987	Precision components
6	Sony Electronics	1988	Hi-fi audio, Walkmans, CD Boomboxes, Discmans
7	Sony TV Industries	1988	CTV, TV tuners, deflection yokes
8	Sony Magnetic Products	1988	Audio tapes
9	Sony Siam Industries	1988	CTV, audio
10	Sony Semiconductor	1989	Bipolar ICs, MOS-ICs
11	Sony Mechatronic Products	1990	3.5" MFDD
12	Sony Video	1990	1/2" VCR, CD-Rom drive
13	PT Sony Electronics Indonesia	1992	Hi-fi audio, Boomboxes, CD Boomboxes
14	Sony Display Device	1992	CRT
15	Shanghai Suogang Electronics	1994	8mm VCR components, optical pick-ups
16	Sony Vietnam	1994	CTV, audio
17	Sony India	1995	CTV

Sony, the Japanese consumer electronics group, will by spring 1997 be making more than 1m mobile telephones a year at an industrial park near Beijing airport.

The $29m joint venture, Sony's first on mainland China, is typical of the new wave of Japanese investment. It is part of a tidal wave of money breaking over many of Japan's Asian neighbours, but increasingly focused on China.

The Beijing mobile phone project follows a video cassette recorder joint venture launched in Shanghai last year and foreshadows two or three more Chinese projects under negotiation, says Mr Kenji Tamiya, Sony's senior managing director.

The potential political and financial risks of investing in China are huge, but Sony, like others, can no longer afford to be hyper-cautious about entering a market of more than 1bn people whose demand for consumer electronics is growing at roughly 20 per cent a year.

East Asia, including China, is a "goldmine for existing products," he says.Sony's experience in East Asia well illustrates the Japanese investment trend in the region. First cautious steps into local assembly of largely imported components for export to third countries have been followed by ever-larger investments using higher proportions of locally-made components for assembly into products for the local market, exports to other Asian countries, the US and, increasingly, back to Japan.

For Sony's investment in the region, the main driving force has been the fast growth of east Asian markets themselves, now expanding at 15–20 per cent a year; the fastest growing region in the world. Over the past decade, Sony's sales in the region have grown from 6 per cent to 20 per cent of the group total.

Sony first set foot in east Asia in April 1967, almost by chance, when the acquisition of another Japanese company happened to include a radio and telephone producing unit in Taiwan. Its second step into the region, a television tuner factory in South Korea, also came as the result of an acquisition in 1973.

Then came a nine-year gap, during which Sony made no east Asian investments, focusing instead on its home ground. That was understandable, in a period when the Japanese domestic market was experiencing the kind of growth only now seen among Asian high flyers.

A Malaysian radio, Walkman and telephone plant opened in 1984 –: Sony's first greenfield plant in Asia –: followed by a video cassette recorder factory in Taiwan in the same year. But the dam did not really burst until after the 1985 Plaza Accord, when the world's leading economies agreed to co-operate to devalue an over-valued dollar. That was the turning point for the yen, which touched Y263 to the dollar that year and has since moved to around Y100, in the process rendering large swathes of Japanese domestic manufacturing uncompetitive.

Sony, like others, took the only option: to move production offshore, in search of cheaper costs and easier exchange rates. "We just had to do it, to keep our products competitively priced," says Mr Toshiyuki Takinaga, general manager for consumer and audiovisual products.

By the end of the decade, eight more Sony plants were in operation in Singapore, Malaysia and Thailand, since when they have been joined by five more –: in Indonesia , Singapore, China, Vietnam and India.

Now, 25,000 of Sony's 138,000 employees are in Asia, within which Malaysia counts the highest number of staff –: 18,500 –:of any single country outside Japan. Local content is high, up to 97 per cent for video recorders and televisions in Malaysia.

Another factor in Sony's Asian expansion was the desirability of avoiding high import duties on assembled goods. Local assembly of imported parts was the obvious answer, as Sony and many other Japanese companies also discovered in Europe –: one factor in the rapid growth in the 1980s of Japanese investment there.

William Dawkins

Review

11 Read **5.8**.
   a Identify four reasons why Sony has set up branch plants in SE Asia.
   b Identify two changes that have occurred in Sony's investment in SE Asia.
   c How are Sony's operations helping to create interdependence within SE Asia?
   d What was the significance of the 1985 Plaza Accord?

Dependence or interdependence?

In the last two sections we have looked at the relationships between the economic giant Japan and four countries that are well behind on the development path. That development gap almost inevitably results in the relationship being one of dependence rather than interdependence. The harsh nature of the economic world is such that the strong exploit the weak – there is little compassion. Even aid programmes, with their loans and consequent debt, seem intended to maintain that inequality. Despite its emphasis on economic cooperation between member states, dependence persists even within ASEAN. Remember also that Japan is not the only country tapping the resources of lower middle-income economies. The Tigers, the USA and the UK are among the interested parties. So dependence is another feature that we might add to the list of development descriptors of lower middle-income economies put together in **Section C.**

The best hope for the lower middle-income nations is that they may ultimately gain strength from the very act of having their resources and business opportunities exploited, albeit by others. At least, they can begin to pick up power from the development cable and make progress. As a consequence, they have a chance of narrowing the gap between themselves and those countries presently tapping their resources. This in turn may be expected to slowly reduce the degree of dependence. In the longer-term, perhaps, relationships with these more advanced countries may even begin to turn towards interdependence. However, the prospects of ever achieving genuine equality and equal benefits must remain very remote.

Enquiry

1   Find out about Indonesia's disputes in Timor and Irian Jaya.

2   a Identify ways in which the physical geography of Indonesia differs from that of Malaysia.
    b From the point of view of development, which of these two countries do you think has the more difficult physical geography ?

3   From which other countries do the four lower middle-income countries receive aid?

4   a What primary products are being exported from ASEAN countries to Japan?
    b Rank them in terms of relative value.

5   Find out what has happened to the values of ASEAN currencies and its financial markets since 1997.

6   a Visit a local travel agent and find out about package holidays to one of the lower middle-income countries.
    b Where are the tourist destinations in your chosen country?
    c Which resources is tourism actively exploiting?
    d What would you identify as (i) the opportunities and (ii) the constraints in any future expansion of tourism?

7   Referring to **4.3** and **5.2**, what differences do you identify between the Tigers and the lower middle-income countries?

8   'The move from dependence to interdependence is an indicator of development.' To what extent do you agree with this statement?

The backmarkers: Cambodia, Laos, North Korea and Vietnam

Introduction

In this chapter, analysis turns to four of the low-income economies of the Asian Pacific region – Cambodia, Laos, North Korea and Vietnam (1.5). The first and last of these, along with China, are sometimes termed 'transitional economies'; i.e. they are moving away from hard-line socialism towards a more market-oriented socialism. Recent developments in each of the four countries will be identified and explained. This will be followed by an analysis that tries to draw from the case studies answers to two key questions:

- What are the reasons for the retarded development of these countries?
- What of the future?

Figure 6.1 Indochina and its three communist states

Case study: Vietnam

The physical geography of Vietnam is not helpful to national unity. It consists of two major deltas – those of the Mekong and the Red River – linked only by a narrow coastal strip backed by a mountainous spine. Vietnam was part of French Indochina from 1884 until the ending of French colonial rule in 1954, when the country was divided into North and South, each part focused on one of the deltas. But it was to be more than mountains that separated the two halves. North Vietnam aligned itself with the former Soviet Union, South Vietnam with the West. This arrangement led fairly swiftly to confrontation and the highly destructive Vietnam War (1957–75). The USA played a major part in this war, as part of its global strategy to stem the southward spread of communism. Victory was eventually secured by North Vietnam in 1976, when the whole country was reunited as the Socialist Republic of Vietnam under a rigid Soviet-style government based in the North's capital city, Hanoi.

For the next ten years, Vietnam was isolated from the global community and its economy declined. This was a period of widespread poverty and unrest. Gradually, it became painfully apparent that the whole approach to the economy needed to change:

- collective agriculture was abandoned;
- private ownership of land was reintroduced;
- private factories were encouraged;
- foreign investment was invited in (6.3);
- government control was relaxed in favour of market forces.

Since 1985 Vietnam has certainly made progress. The current economic strategy aims by the year 2000 to:

- double per capita income;
- raise rice production;
- triple electricity production;
- boost exports.

Between 1985 and 1995 per capita GNP grew at an average annual rate of 4.2 per cent – this raised it to a level of $240 per capita. The economy of Vietnam has typically had a strong agricultural base. Today, agriculture and forestry generate a quarter of GDP (6.1). The two deltas, with their dense populations, have always been important rice-growing areas. Since 1985, annual rice production has nearly doubled to 22.3 million tonnes and rice is now exported along with groundnuts, pineapples, bananas and oranges. Rubber is another export commodity.

Figure 6.2 Sectoral shifts in the Vietnamese economy (1985–95)

	1985 (% GDP)	1995 (% GDP)
Agriculture & forestry	36	25
Industry	31	31
Services	33	42

One problem looming large for Vietnam is population pressure. The present population of nearly 75 million is growing at a rate of 2.2 per cent per annum. The prospects for expansion of agricultural production are extremely limited, as forested land cover has already been reduced to less than 30 per cent and there is little forested land left that is capable of being transformed into fields.

Vietnam's mineral base is mainly located in the north and includes coal, salt, iron, tin, zinc, lead and phosphates. Iron and steel, cement, fertilisers and chemicals are industrial products derived from these resources. Other significant manufactures are textiles, sugar and paper. But 6.2 clearly shows the industrial sector to be somewhat stagnant as regards its contribution to GDP. It is the service sector that appears to be on the up.

As for trade, exports include craft goods such as embroidery and leather. Imports are dominated by oil, motor vehicles, machines, spare parts and textile raw materials. However, the recent discovery of offshore oil deposits could alter the composition of imports.

With the break-up of the Soviet Union, Vietnam lost its minder and backer. For this and other reasons, it has had to end its policy of isolation. Increasing involvement in world trade and growing foreign investment are signs of this change, as was its becoming a member of ASEAN in 1995 (see **Chapter 5**). **6.3** gives some information about this foreign investment, a substantial part of which comes from within the Asian Pacific region. Analysis shows that two-thirds of this investment is focused on the three leading urban centres: Ho Chi Minh City, Hanoi and Dong-nai. These three cores are creating a huge periphery.

Figure 6.3 Foreign investment in Vietnam (as of 1995)

	No. of projects	Capital ($ million)
Taiwan	219	3 226.9
Hong Kong	178	2 212.3
Japan	110	1 688.4
Singapore	108	1 474.2
South Korea	127	1 415.9
USA	44	995.2
Malaysia	41	826.3
Australia	48	715.4
France	68	627.5
Total	**1 262**	**16 964.0**

Vietnam today faces a number of challenges that have a direct impact on development. They are:

- how to make the economy more market-oriented without the government losing firm control over it;
- how to ease the lasting tensions and disparity between the north and south of the country – with government based in the north, the south feels neglected;
- how to take advantage of foreign investment and aid without eroding the country's independence.

A major issue is whether it is possible to bring about economic reforms without also implementing political reforms. Clearly, Vietnam has achieved some progress over the last ten years or so, but it is doubtful whether significant additional progress will ever be achieved with the present communist government. State-owned enterprise is still responsible for 40 per cent of GDP.

Review

1 a Draw a flow map showing the origins and amounts of foreign investment being made in Vietnam (6.2).
   b Suggest reasons why Taiwan and Hong Kong are larger investors in Vietnam than Japan.
2 Which of the three challenges outlined in the penultimate paragraph do you think is going to prove the most difficult? Justify your viewpoint.

Case study: Cambodia (Kampuchea)

At the end of the 1980s much of Cambodia lay in ruins. It had been devastated by internal warfare and misrule. The initial conflict had been between its military government and the Cambodian communists (the Khmer Rouge). In 1975 the latter won power and created a extreme regime that emptied the cities and suppressed all opposition. Approximately two and a half million people died or were killed. In 1978 Vietnam invaded the country and set about removing the Khmer Rouge, a task which was not completed until 1985. Four years later the Vietnamese forces withdrew and so Cambodia was left to pick up the pieces of nearly two decades of destruction and neglect.

Since 1989, Cambodia has gradually shaken itself free of communism and become a democracy. In May 1993 free elections took place. It now has a parliamentary system, an elected government (albeit a fragile coalition) and a constitutional monarch as head of state. Ties with the international community, from which Cambodia had become isolated, are being restored. As a consequence, the country is now receiving aid from donor countries. A rising deficit in its budget is being met only by an increased supply of foreign money. With the move to democracy, so the transition to a market economy has begun.

Figure 6.4 Sectoral shifts in the Cambodian economy

	1991 (% GDP)	1995 (% GDP)
Agriculture	43.5	38.1
Fishing	5.1	3.8
Forestry	3.3	2.7
Mining	1.1	1.2
Manufacturing	7.2	7.6
Construction	6.7	9.9
Services	33.1	36.7

Cambodia consists mainly of a huge lowland, across which flows the Mekong River. Its productive resources are modest – largely agriculture, fishing and forestry. **6.4** shows some shifting in the sectoral balance between 1991 and 1995. Even so, the primary sector still accounts for over 45 per cent of GDP. By far the most important crop is rice, but crops such as jute and rubber are also grown for industrial use. There is much land suited to rice production, particularly within the catchment of the Mekong, but one-third of it is currently not used. Yields are relatively low for the following reasons:

- poor soil fertility;
- poor water control;
- lack of a sustainable pest-control programme;
- precipitation varies from year to year;
- limited availability of improved seeds;
- lack of draft animals.

Review

3 a Represent the data in **6.4** by means of an appropriate diagram.
  b How does the sectoral shift in Cambodia compare with that in Vietnam (**6.2**)?

4 What conclusions do you draw from **6.6**?

Rubber and timber have for many years been Cambodia's most important export commodities, currently accounting for nearly 75 per cent of total exports. Other primary sector products, such as cattle, rice, fruit and fish, are also traded to neighbouring countries. Clearly, the future development of Cambodia is going to depend on reforms and progress being made in rural areas and particularly in agriculture. The challenge will be to move towards sustainable rural development.

There has been a strong increase in foreign direct investment since 1993. There are several reasons why foreign investors find Cambodia attractive:

- the cost of labour is very low;
- the country's location makes it well suited as a base from which to serve the Greater Mekong subregion;
- the government offers very generous incentives to foreign investors;
- the bureaucracy associated with investment is considered less irksome than in Vietnam;
- real estate can be leased for up to 70 years, although never purchased.

Most foreign investors to date have come from Malaysia, Singapore, China and Thailand. The sectors that attract most interest are textiles, services, construction, oil and wood products.

There are two big obstacles to Cambodia's development. First, there is the continuing strife between political factions. Secondly, there is its high level of external indebtedness that has accumulated over the years, principally as a result of receiving foreign aid (**6.5**). Cambodia's current accumulated debt is equivalent to roughly 80 per cent of GDP and is rising. In 1995 Cambodia tried to obtain relief on its debts. Some aid donors agreed, but Russia, which is owed something like three-quarters of the total debt, refused to enter into negotiations. This well illustrates the dilemma of so many less-developed countries. Do they go it alone slowly, or do they take the faster development route of loans and dependency on others?

Thus the prospects are that the Cambodian economy will continue to be undermined by its debt burden and internal unrest. Despite recent improvements in the economy's performance, Cambodia remains one of the poorest countries in the world. In fact, Cambodia today is only a little better off than in the late 1960s, before the traumatic events of the 1970s and 1980s (**6.6**). Some social indicators are better now, but per capita income still has yet not fully recovered.

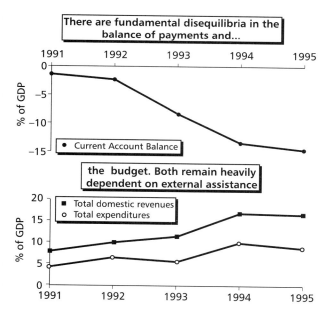

Figure 6.5 Development assistance or descent into debt?

	1970	1995
Life expectancy (years)	42	52
Crude death rate	20	15
Adult literacy (% of pop)	36	65
Primary education (% of pop)	77	53

Figure 6.6 Cambodia – some social indicators

Case study: Laos

Laos People's Republic is the one country of the Asian Pacific region not to front the Pacific Ocean. It is a landlocked and elongated state squeezed between China, Thailand, Cambodia, Myanmar and Vietnam (6.1). Its terrain is dominated by mountain ranges and plateaux. The valley of the Mekong provides some of the most usable land, but the river also forms the sensitive border with much of Thailand. Remoteness and poverty are two key features.

In 1893 Laos became a French protectorate. Some 50 years later communist insurgents began to destabilise the country. In 1949 the country won independence within the French Union; five years later it became completely independent. However, continuous rivalry between right- and left-wing factions led to many years of unrest and eventually to intervention by the great powers. Gradually, the left-wing faction gained the upper hand. In 1975 Laos became a centrally-planned economy with government control and ownership of productive enterprises. Since 1986, however, efforts have been made to transform the economy to a more open market-based system.

Subsistence agriculture remains the main occupation, accounting for 55 per cent of GDP and providing about 85 per cent of total employment. The dominant crop is rice, but with low yields and an unreliable climate there is often a shortfall in food. Industry and handicrafts generate around 20 per cent of GDP and services 25 per cent. Rich iron ore deposits have been discovered, but only tin ore is exploited commercially. The main problem is inaccessibility, since there are no railways and few roads. Timber, wood-based products and HEP are currently the biggest legitimate earners of foreign currency. Opium is an illicit commodity. Two-thirds of the population live in rural areas; there are few sizeable urban centres. Telecommunications and electricity are available only in limited areas.

There is a recurrent deficit in the national budget; in some years it is equivalent to 10 per cent of GDP. The deficit is financed largely through external assistance, mainly from the International Monetary Fund, and foreign investment. 6.7 looks at the sectoral allocation and origins of the latter. It is surprising not to find Japan among the top ten investors; this may reflect Japanese caution and the perception that Laos is still a high-risk investment area. Interestingly, Laos has recently applied for membership of ASEAN.

A major challenge confronting Laos is deforestation and environmental degradation caused by illegal logging and shifting cultivation. Natural resources and biodiversity are threatened. So too is the chance for many rural communities to have sustainable and secure livelihoods.

Review

5 Study 6.7 and write an analytical account of the targets and sources of foreign investment in Laos.

Ranking	Sector	No of projects	% of total investment	Country	No of projects	% of total investment
1	Electricity	7	66.3	Thailand	233	44.8
2	Tourism	34	8.9	USA	39	29.1
3	Transport	13	8.3	S. Korea	17	7.8
4	Handicraft	115	7	France	68	6.2
5	Wood	36	2.4	Malaysia	11	3.7
6	Mining	28	1.7	Australia	41	2.6
7	Finance	11	1.1	Taiwan	31	1.3
8	Clothing	75	1.1	Norway	1	1.1
9	Construction	35	0.9	China	61	0.8
10	Agribusiness	65	0.8	UK	13	0.6

Figure 6.7 Foreign investment in Laos (1988–97)

Case study: North Korea

The Democratic People's Republic of Korea, as it is properly known, vies with Laos in being the most isolated state of the Asian Pacific region. It is also distinguished by a dearth of official statistics, a massaging of those few that are released, and a general clamp-down on any information about what is really going on in the country. Because of all this, the following discussion is brief and at times speculative.

The partition of the Korean peninsula took place in 1948 after its recapture from the Japanese at the end of the Second World War. From the outset, there was tension between the two parts – North Korea had a communist government and a centrally-planned economy, South Korea a democratic government and a market economy. That tension flared into the Korean War (1950–53) when the communists tried to annexe South Korea. For some 45 years now the two states have glared at each other across the demilitarised zone that keeps them a part.

North Korea occupies slightly more of the peninsula than South Korea, but its population of 24 million is only just over half that of its neighbour. Agriculture has been and remains a significant part of the North Korean economy. There is rather more lowland than in South Korea and the climate is generally favourable. Rice and other cereals are its main outputs, along with livestock. However, rigid adoption of the collective system has failed to raise production to a sufficient degree. This, in combination with population growing at a rate 1.8 per cent per annum and a succession of poor harvests, has led to severe food shortages (**6.9**).

North Korea possesses quite good resources of coal and lignite, iron ore, magnetite and tungsten. Much of its industrialisation has been related to working these resources, as for example by the iron and steel industry. Metal products, chemicals and cement are among manufactured goods that figure in exports.

A new agency offers the experience of a lifetime, says Harvey Elliott

Britons start tours to North Korea

TWO British entrepreneurs are opening up one of the world's most isolated and secretive countries to Western tourists.

Nicholas Bonner, 35, and Josh Green, 29, have formed a travel agency in Peking, specialising in tours to North Korea. They are already inundated with requests for details of the trips which include Pyongyang, the capital, and Panmunjom.

Mr Bonner is enthusiastic about the country, which is dominated by giant statues of "The Great Leader" Kim Il Sung but which, he insists is "one of the safest on earth", adding: "It is a very serious country and one where the taking of pictures, for example, is very restricted. But visitors who arrive with preconceived ideas find that the people are open and friendly, the architecture is staggering and the opportunity of seeing a society that is so completely different, and that somehow puts everything we treasure in the West into context, just has to be grabbed now. North Korea has adopted a slightly more relaxed attitude towards tourism and 1997 is the year to visit the 'People's Paradise'."

Figure 6.8 Wishful thinking, or a real development possibility?

North Korea, like the South, has a population that is ethnically 99 per cent Korean. In explaining the economic success of South Korea, attention was drawn to certain vital qualities of the Koreans **(Chapter 4)**. It must be a great embarrassment to the political leaders of North Korea that the same type of labour and better natural resources have failed to produce anything like the scale of development enjoyed by South Korea. The difference stands as an indictment of the centrally-planned economy: its distrust of private enterprise, and its wastage of resources on military forces and showpiece projects that do little or nothing to improve the lot of the people **(6.8)**.

The contrasts either side of the demilitarised zone could not be sharper. While North Korea faces poverty and stagnation, South Korea grapples with the problems of economic success. At present, the economy of North Korea is only 13 per cent the size of that of South Korea; an estimated per capita GNP of less than $1 000 compares with a figure of $7 670. To the outside world, the situation cries out for reunification. Without doubt, the complementarity of the two parts would generate development benefits for those living on both sides of the demilitarised

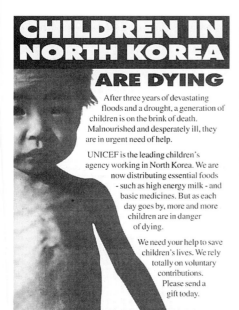

CHILDREN IN NORTH KOREA ARE DYING

After three years of devastating floods and a drought, a generation of children is on the brink of death. Malnourished and desperately ill, they are in urgent need of help.

UNICEF is the leading children's agency working in North Korea. We are now distributing essential foods - such as high energy milk - and basic medicines. But as each day goes by, more and more children are in danger of dying.

We need your help to save children's lives. We rely totally on voluntary contributions. Please send a gift today.

zone. The marrying of North Korea's natural resources and cheap labour with South Korea's human resources and economic systems could be quite formidable. Sadly, the only real chance of that ever happening would be if there were some profound political change in North Korea. That prospect seems highly remote. For the moment, aid organisations are running appeals to help feed starving North Koreans. The causes of that hunger are more deep-rooted than 'three years of devastating floods' **(6.9)**. This is only part of the explanation for the North Korea's contracting economy **(1.5)**.

Review

6 Provide a reasoned answer to the question posed by the caption to **6.8**.
7 Make a list of the factors that you think may have contributed to the famine in North Korea **(6.9)**.

Figure 6.9 The plight of North Korea

SECTION C

Why are these countries so retarded?

Having looked at these four case-studies, we now need to address two questions:

- What development features do they appear to have in common?
- What factors might help explain their low-income status?

Six relevant features may be identified.

- All four are small countries (i.e. smaller even than Japan) **(1.6)**; only North Korea is well endowed with natural resources. However, the example of the four Tigers suggests that these features need not be serious disadvantages. Indeed, smallness might even be a positive advantage, and good human resources seem quite capable of providing adequate compensation for poor physical resources.
- In terms of these countries' economic sectors, agriculture and other primary activities account for a larger share of GDP than in more developed countries. Manufacturing, such as it is, is export-oriented rather than geared to import-substitution. The low levels of personal affluence inevitably mean these countries have restricted service sectors.
- Foreign investors are being welcomed by two of the countries. Investment seems to be particularly drawn by the presence of natural resources and cheap labour.

These first three features are of an essentially positive character that give reasons to be hopeful for the future. The next three are more negative and as such help to account for the retarded development.

- All four have suffered as battlefields during the second half of the 20th century. North Korea was fought over in the early 1950s, Vietnam, Laos and Cambodia in the 1960s and 1970s. There is no denying the debilitating effects of war: the destruction of infrastructure, the loss of people and the wastage of material resources are but three of a wide range.

- All four countries have for decades been ruled by communist governments. It may well be that under communism, development is seen in a rather different way and as having different aims. Perhaps it is that communism does not give high priority to economic growth or the material condition of people? Or perhaps it is that communism is in some way flawed and incapable of delivering development at the pace quite clearly achieved by market economies?

- Internal tensions within Cambodia, Laos and Vietnam continue to simmer. The longer they do so, the more they are likely to handicap development. The same is probably true of North Korea, but here a heavy-handed government has thus far managed to keep the lid on things.

The general collapse of communism elsewhere in the world at the end of the 1980s threatened to increase the isolation of these remaining communist states. With fewer such regimes around, so opportunities to cooperate and trade internationally have contracted. The case studies of Japan and the Tigers quite clearly show that in today's world these external links are critical to development. Japan seems to have adopted a cautious approach in terms of opening up trade, investment and aid links with these countries. At present, it looks as if Vietnam might be the most favoured of these countries.

Enquiry

1 Investigate collective farming. What were seen as its advantages? What were its failings?

2 Try to find out what has been happening in each of these four countries since 1995.

3 **a** Which of the four communist countries examined in this chapter do you think has most to offer Japan?
b Explain why Japan is being cautious in opening up links with these countries.

4 Write an essay entitled 'Debt and development in the Asian Pacific region'.

This is the age of the global economy. Today's communist countries must choose between confining their contacts to the diminishing number of nations of the same ideological frame of mind, or forgetting the ideology and seeking out those overseas contacts that promise the best returns. At the time of writing, it would seem that only North Korea has opted for the former, and that Cambodia, Laos and Vietnam (like China) are moving towards the latter. Perhaps that difference in choice will create a widening development gap between the two camps? There is also a parallel choice – whether to seek outside assistance with development, or to go it alone? The former promises faster progress, but also debt and dependence. The latter, however, may mean slipping further behind and even less hope of ever entering into an interdependent relationship with the outside world. These countries would seem to have limited options.

The awakening giant: China

SECTION A

Introduction

China is the fifth member of the low-income grouping of countries. If only because of its geographical dimensions, it warrants a separate chapter. China is a giant of a country: it is nearly 40 times the size of the UK and accounts for one-fifth of the world's population **(1.6)**. Not surprisingly, the country contains a diversity of physical environments, ranging from very high mountain to coastal lowland, from steppe to humid subtropical. A varied agriculture and food supply are obvious benefits of such diversity. China is also well endowed with energy resources (coal, oil, natural gas and abundant HEP potential). Its mineral base includes iron ore, bauxite, tungsten, tin and lead.

Despite its wealth of resources, however, China is still a long way short of the state of development reached by Japan and the other advanced economies. But that is beginning to change and during the last two decades China has made clear progress along the development pathway. Whatever happens in China is almost inevitably going to be of immense significance to the rest of the Asian Pacific region, if not to the world as a whole.

In this chapter, a particular aim is to discover whether the character of the development process is any different in China as compared with other Asian Pacific countries. There are two factors that might lead us to suspect this could be the case: China's huge size and its well-entrenched communist government.

The modern state of China came into being in 1949 as a result of a communist insurrection led by Mao Zedong. Since then the country has gone through various types of communist rule, from the bizarre and purging Cultural Revolution of the 1960s to the more 'liberal' and reforming government of today. Despite the current brand of market socialism, the government of China remains undemocratic, authoritarian and repressive. Although there has been a programme of privatisation, the state retains complete control over the economy. Despite the collapse of the Soviet Union and communist rule in Eastern Europe, China seems set on remaining a communist state. Does this make China a dinosaur, or the pioneer of a some new mode of development?

SECTION B

The current state of play

One of the frustrations of studying China and the few remaining communist states concerns statistical information. Data either are not

	GDP %
Agriculture	19
Manufacturing	38
Services	33
Others	10

Figure 7.1 The sectors of the Chinese economy (1995)

available, or have to be treated with suspicion. Massaging statistics is something that communist states have proved themselves to be good at.

In 1995 GNP in China was about one-seventh that of the Japanese economy, but nearly double that of the South Korean economy (**1.5**). Expressed in per capita terms, China's economic performance is shown to be very weak. The per capita figure was dwarfed by those of Japan and even South Korea. Nonetheless, during the period 1985 to 1995, per capita GNP grew at a mean annual rate of 6.5 per cent.

Agriculture

It is estimated that 80 per cent of China's huge population are rural. For this reason alone, the Chinese economy and the development drive are closely linked to agriculture. Whilst around 70 per cent of all jobs are in agriculture, the sector generates about 20 per cent of GDP (**7.1**). This importance of agriculture is a feature that clearly distinguishes the Chinese economy from the high- and higher middle-income economies. If for this reason alone, progress in agriculture must be central to the wider development of the country, that is until exports of goods can be used to buy in food from overseas.

The challenge of raising levels of food production is made difficult by two features of China's physical geography:

- the acute shortage of good arable land; there are few opportunities for extending the cultivated area to more than the present 10 per cent of the total land area;
- the shortage and unreliability of precipitation over much of China.

On the organisational side, family farming has returned, collectives have been abandoned and market systems introduced (**7.2**). The effects on production and rural income have been modest. China seems to have reached the critical point where, unless the amount of food produced is increased and the number of people required to produce it falls, the brake will be put on further urbanisation and industrialisation.

Figure 7.2 One of China's challenges – to raise agricultural productivity

Industry

Manufacturing currently generates 38 per cent of China's GDP, but the industrial sector as a whole (i.e. including mining, construction and public utilities) accounts for almost half (**7.1**). There has been a fundamental change in the character of manufacturing over the last 20 years. Previously, the emphasis had been on heavy industry (for example, steel, chemicals and cement) and using labour-intensive methods. Today, light industries producing consumer goods and processing agricultural materials are much more in evidence. Indeed, the value of their output is roughly the same as that of heavy industry. The shift has been brought about by a number of important reforms:

- gradually abandoning state ownership of industry and allowing private companies to take over;
- introducing an open-door policy that encourages foreign investment and joint ventures with foreign companies (**see Section C**);
- reinstating a market mechanism.

The shift has also been encouraged by a steady rise in consumer spending. But the industrial sector still has its challenges, such as:

- modernising factories and production methods;
- reducing government subsidies to state-owned enterprises;
- abandoning the two-tier price-system in the purchasing of materials and the selling of output, whereby prices in the state sector are held lower than those in the private sector.

Services

Generating only one-third of GDP, the Chinese tertiary sector is very much in its infancy compared with more advanced economies (**7.1**). The situation is, however, beginning to change. Increased agricultural and industrial output, together with rising trade, are creating demand for more commercial services like banking and insurance (**7.3**). An upward movement in wages is leading to more consuming spending and therefore more retailing. Rising expectations as to the quality of life are calling for more social services – schools, libraries and hospitals – as well as the growth of the mass-media. All these movements provide fuel for the enlargement of the tertiary sector .

Figure 7.3 The links between services and growth in the other economic sectors

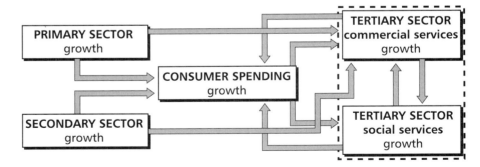

Review

1 Compare the sectoral balance of China's economy with those of Japan and the Tigers (**2.2**, **4.3** and **7.1**).

2 In the case of China's development, do you think that its huge territory is a hindrance or a help?

3 In your own words, explain the links shown in **7.3**.

Second World meets First World

A key feature of China's current approach to development is its 'open-door' policy. Perhaps surprisingly, the policy reaches out to those advanced economies that together make up the so-called First World. By inviting foreign investment and encouraging joint ventures with overseas companies, the pace of China's economic growth is speeded up. Capital and technology are the two things that China desperately needs. Leading investors from the Asian Pacific region are Japan, Taiwan and Hong Kong; businesses from the UK and USA are also active in China. In addition, China is receiving loans from the World Bank, the Asian Development Bank and the Japanese Overseas Development Agency.

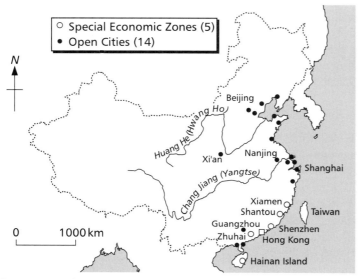

Figure 7.4 The distribution of foreign investment in China

In this internationalisation of the Chinese economy, it is interesting to note the operation of so-called 'guanxi networks'. Guanxi refers to the connections that exist between Chinese people and companies scattered around the world. The connections can be to do with family and clan; equally they can be to do with sharing the same ancestors in a particular province back in China. Basically, guanxi networks allow Chinese entrepreneurs to operate internationally. It is clear, for example, that such networks are behind much of the investment entering China from Hong Kong, Taiwan and Singapore, and perhaps even from the USA and UK.

A final feature of the open-door policy is the concentration of foreign investment and activity in selected areas of E and SE China (**7.4**). These take the form of 14 'open' coastal cities, where special tax incentives are offered to foreign investment and trade. Then there are the five Special Economic Zones (SEZs) – one in Hainan Province, three in Guangdong and one in Fujian – where even more tempting concessions are on offer to outsiders. Investors from Hong Kong and Taiwan have been drawn by two factors – labour that is at least 80 per cent cheaper than in Hong Kong, and land that is up one-third the price. These SEZs have been remarkably successful. With their booming economies they represent the most prosperous parts of China today. The return of Hong Kong to Chinese rule in 1997 may be of considerable benefit to the SEZs in neighbouring Guangdong Province, particularly Shenzhen. The hope is that they will function as growth poles from which development will trickle down to adjacent areas. All this promises well for coastal China, but the official policy has been to protect the rest of China from contact with the West. The outcome seems certain to be spatial disparities in development of such severity that they are likely to threaten the creation of two Chinas.

Review

4 Using a suitable proportional symbol, plot the investment statistics in **4.10** on a tracing of the map of Chinese provinces. Write a brief account summarising the features of the distribution.

China and Japan

Such a study might be subtitled 'a tale of two giants' – China by virtue of its size and resources, Japan because of its economic wealth and global influence. Although the two countries stand as the status symbols of two very different ideologies – communism and capitalism – the links between the two countries go back centuries. Indeed, many important aspects of Japanese culture were derived from China. The relationship has fluctuated between outright hostility and peaceful coexistence and now seems to be making the transition from the former to the latter. Yet there are people still alive in China today who remember Japan's annexation of the province of Manchuria in 1930 and invasion of much of China during the Second World War.

There are three ways in which Japan is currently helping China's development – trade, investment and aid. But those three links do, of course, benefit Japan. Japan is not in the business of giving charity, and China would never wish to be seen receiving it.

Figure 7.5 Trade between China and Japan (1981–96)

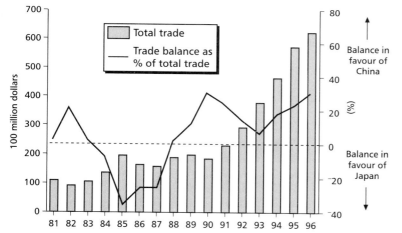

Trade

China has for some time traded more with Japan than any other nation. In 1995 it became Japan's second most important trading partner. **7.5** shows a marked rise in the total value of trade in the 1990s as the balance of trade began to tip increasingly in China's favour. In 1996 the surplus in China's favour was worth nearly $19 billion. The main commodities involved in that trade are shown in **7.6**.

China's imports from Japan (% by value)		China's exports to Japan (% by value)	
General machinery	29.1	Textile products	33.6
Electrical machinery	21.1	Machinery	18.1
Textile materials	11.9	Foodstuffs	12.5
Chemical products	9.4	Mineral fuels	5.9
Iron & steel	7.6	Metal products	3.7
Transport equipment	4.2	Raw materials	3.6
Precision instrument	2.4	Chemical products	3.5
Others	14.3	Others	19.1

Figure 7.6 The main commodities in China–Japan trade (1996)

Investment

Reference has already been made to the Special Economic Zones as the main recipients of foreign investment in China. So far, Japan has shown a conspicuous presence in only two of those zones – Shanghai and Shenzhen (**7.4** and **7.7**). Much of the Japanese investment in China is being undertaken elsewhere by its multinational companies like Matsushita. Also significant in this context are the large inter-bank loans that have been agreed between the Export-Import Bank of Japan and the Bank of China. These loans are essentially long-term and low-interest. To date, they have helped to finance the opening of several large oilfields and a number of huge coal mines. Current Chinese plans for boosting agricultural and industrial output by the turn of the century depend critically on greatly increasing energy supplies. Coal and oil are two Chinese commodities that also happen to interest the Japanese.

Figure 7.7 The location of Japanese investment in China (1992)

City	No. of projects	Value of projects ($ million)
Dalian	394	1 188
Shanghai	339	810
Beijing	340	121
Tianjin	262	367
Shenzhen	183	555

Case study: Matsushita in China

Matsushita, the world's largest electronics company, broke new ground in November, 1996 by opening its first research and development centre in China. This move is just one example of how the overseas investment plans of Japanese multinational companies have accelerated sharply in the past five years and have switched direction towards Asian emerging markets. They have been pushed by the yen's strength on the one hand, and pulled by East Asia's fast economic growth. At the same time, Japanese foreign investments have 'moved upstream', from simple assembly to more sophisticated business functions.

The yen's decline from a peak of 80 yen to the US dollar in April 1995 to its present level of around 100 has caused some Japanese manufacturers, like Toyota, Honda and Aiwa, to modify their foreign investment plans, bringing some production back home to make use of newly competitive spare capacity there. But this has not, on the evidence of Matsushita and others, halted the long-term exodus of Japanese manufacturers from Japan's mature and over-regulated economy to higher growth and more open markets in neighbouring parts of the Asian Pacific region.

Five years ago, China was little more than a convenient base for Matsushita's low-cost assembly of commodity products for re-export to Japan, Europe and the USA. The sorts of products include air conditioners, TV tubes, etc. The big change now is that Matsushita's Chinese arm makes high-tech VCR components in Shanghai and sells most of its output to the domestic market and to SE Asian neighbours. It is also researching new multimedia technologies in Beijing, the type of activity Matsushita previously reserved for its skilled workforce back home. The company now has 190 overseas research laboratories.

Figure 7.8 Steam locomotives replaced by electric on the Guangzhou – Shanghai Railway

Aid

Japan first extended bilateral aid to China in 1981. China rapidly became the top recipient and today accounts for about 15 per cent of Japanese overseas development assistance, approximately 80 per cent of which is in the form of loans. Japan now provides more aid to China than any other country. The great bulk of this money has been used to finance infrastructural projects such as the building of a freeport on Hainan Island, installing a modern communications system, building HEP stations and electrifying China's railway network **(7.8)**.

Japanese technical assistance has been almost wholly directed to the modernisation of factories. The small amount of grant aid has been used for such things as building and equipping hospitals, supplying library equipment and educational aids.

Motives

The very idea of Japan apparently helping a country belonging to a different political camp, and of China being willing to accept that help, raises two obvious questions:

- What does Japan expect to gain from China?
- What does China really want from Japan?

The answers lie partly in the physical closeness of the two countries and the fact that each is able to supply what the other lacks. Economically, Japan looks to China as a huge and untapped market for its manufactured goods. Japan is also keen to tap China's oil and coal resources, as part of its strategic wish to diversify its energy sources. China looks to Japan as a market for these fuels. Above all else, though, China looks to Japan for modern technology. Access to Japanese manufactured goods is of secondary importance, and what China prefers to buy is not consumer goods, but capital goods to be used in its own factories **(7.6)**.

There are other motives, too. Japan is anxious to encourage China's development, because in its view a prosperous China is more likely to buy

Japanese goods. At the same time, if China's aspirations to become a major industrial power are realised, then it should be able to satisfy its own demand for consumer goods. The sooner it has the industrial know-how, the sooner China can fulfil its ambitions.

Japan's willingness to cooperate with China has an important political motivation. Japan recognises that its own security and continuing prosperity are closely tied up with the well-being of China. Good relations with a China that is moving slowly and peacefully away from hard-line communism are undoubtedly good for Japan. But relations can be fragile, as shown by the dispute over the ownership of some uninhabited islands lying between Japan, China and Taiwan. At the same time, interaction with Japan has posed some ideological problems for China. Rather than admitting to the superiority of a 'capitalist' economy, China's propaganda machine presents Japanese aid and investment as reparation payments. They are compensating the considerable damage done to the country by the Japanese invasion during the Second World War.

A final point about the character of the broad relationship between the two countries is that it is much more one of interdependence than is the case in most of Japan's other overseas partnerships. On the one hand, this is surprising, given the present wide development gap that separates the two. On the other hand, it may be simply that there is a genuine complementarity here. Or might it be that the meeting of two giants produces a more even match?

Review

5 Using the information in **7.6**, write an account of the commodities being traded between China and Japan.
6 Why do you think Japan prefers to extend aid in the form of loans rather than grants and technical assistance?

SECTION E

A regional linchpin

Because of its size, China has to be seen as a linchpin of the Asian Pacific region. Much of what happens in China is likely to have repercussions throughout the region. For example, a China that is moving steadily along the development pathway and towards a market socialist economy, interacting with other countries through the peaceful means of economic cooperation, undoubtedly is good for the region. However, a China that is keen to spread subversion and communism would be seriously destabilising and would put at risk the development hopes of all the other countries of the region. These contrasting scenarios underline the importance of international relationships and diplomacy, of peace and cooperation in providing the right conditions for development. They also serve to emphasise the point that players on the international stage are not of equal importance. Some command much more clout than others.

Finally, it is necessary to return briefly to the question posed in the introduction: is China pioneering a distinctive development pathway? It is too early to say. In giving priority to increased agricultural productivity, industrialisation, trade and inward investment, China would seem to be very different. However, given its gentle move towards market socialism and its immense resources, China looks certain to be the first of the communist states to graduate from low-income to lower middle-income status.

1   What similarities and differences do you find in the case-studies of Matsushita (**6.4**) and Sony (**5.9**)?

2   Find out more about one of the Special Economic Zones and one of the Open Cities (**7.4**). (You might contact the Information Service at the Chinese Embassy.)

3   Explain and exemplify why political stability is so important to development.

4   Identify what you think are China's most valuable resources.

5   Explain what you understand by the claim that a complementarity exists between China and Japan.

6   Do you think that the nature and course of development in China is distinctive? Justify your viewpoint.

Conclusions

Development revisited

All that now remains is to return to those key questions posed originally in **Chapter 1 Section F**, and asked in subsequent chapters. What generalisations, if any, can be made about the causes and nature of development? Let us start by revisiting the diagram **(2.4)** that tried to identify some of the key factors in Japan's economic success. Does it fit the experiences of other countries as it stands, or does it need revising?

The exploitation of resources

Development is powered by economic growth and that, in turn, by the exploitation of resources. Clearly it helps if a country has a rich base of natural resources, particularly metals and energy. However, the examples of Hong Kong and Singapore show that the quality of human resources can easily compensate for any shortfall in natural resources. There are development pathways that do not require large amounts of natural resources. Equally, the case of Japan shows that natural resources can be obtained through international trade and the activities of multinational corporations. Modern technology is important in realising the potential of both natural and human resources. So too are enterprise and innovation.

Sectoral shifts

The development stage model, or sector theory, was first put forward nearly 40 years ago **(8.1)**. It recognises six stages in the development of a country or region, each stage being marked by a distinctive trend in the balance of the economic sectors:

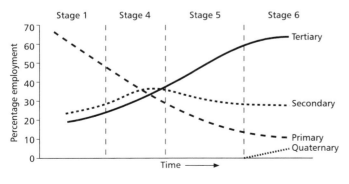

Figure 8.1 The development stage model

- The primary sector is dominant, with an emphasis on self-sufficiency.
- Increased specialisation within the primary sector is accompanied by rising levels of production and the initiation of external trade.
- The secondary sector begins to expand as the processing of primary products creates a small manufacturing base.
- The secondary sector continues to expand. The growth of industrial linkages related to the initial lines of manufacturing leads to industrial diversification.

- Growth in the tertiary sector is generated by increased personal affluence and consumer spending, as well as by increased trade and investment.
- A quaternary sector begins to emerge with more effort being directed towards research and development and the export of new ideas and technology.

Although shifts in the sectoral balance of the economy can be detected in all the case histories, particularly the decline of the primary sector and the rise of the tertiary, few of the more advanced countries appear to have followed the model to any close degree. Perhaps Japan comes closest to replicating the model.

Two basic assumptions of the model must be questioned. First, there is the assumption that development lies rooted in the agricultural sector. Hong Kong and Singapore are two glaring exceptions to this rule. Secondly, the countries examined in this book challenge the traditional view that manufacturing lies at the heart of any acceleration in development. This is not to suggest that the secondary sector is incapable of delivering the large amounts of capital and wealth that energise development. However, in the age of the global economy, countries can and do prosper by providing primary products alone – Brunei is a shining example of that; Thailand and Indonesia less so. The value of being reasonably self-sufficient in food should also not be overlooked. Today, however, it is the diversity of services running the global economy that produces the most potent impetus for development, as the examples of Hong Kong and Singapore clearly demonstrate.

8.2 is a revision of **2.4**. At the one end of the diagram, those things that initiate economic growth are spelt out as energising inputs. Once under way, economic growth is sustained by the same internal and external stimuli that applied in Japan's case. **8.2** also acknowledges that sectoral shifts in the economy are a vital structural element in the development process. They are one of the most important ongoing outcomes. Both these amendments to **2.4** relate to the development cable's core **(1.1)**.

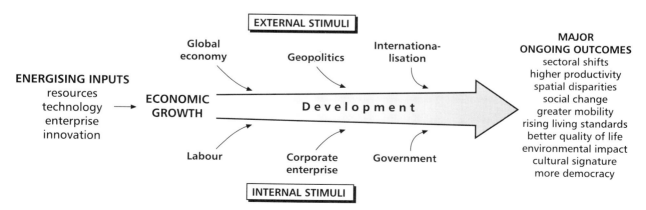

Figure 8.2 Towards a model of development

Government

The important role played by government is something that emerges from all the case studies (8.2). Strong government leadership and intervention have been important in the success of Japan and Singapore. In Hong Kong's case, it was a matter of government providing stability and fidelity in economic institutions such as banks, the stock exchange and the legal system. Equally, though, the examples of the communist countries like Vietnam and Laos show that too much government control or intervention of the wrong kind can easily stifle development.

What comes out in the case studies is the inappropriateness of the simplistic distinction that is often made between democratic, capitalist (free-market) countries with no government intervention, and communist, centrally controlled countries with tough, often repressive governments. Most countries in the Asian Pacific region now occupy positions somewhere along a continuum between these two extremes, where government direction and private enterprise are to be found mixed in varying proportions. What seems to be of critical importance is achieving a good working partnership between the public and private sectors.

Multinational corporations

Although small family enterprises have contributed to the success of the region's high-performing economies, the dominant role has been played by huge multinational corporations (8.2). Because of their breadth of business interests, conglomerates like the Japanese *zaibatsu* or *sogo shosha* (Mitsubishi, Sumitomo, etc.) and the South Korean chaebol (Samsung, Hyundai, etc.) have been a driving force not only in the expansion of manufacturing and commerce at home. What is perhaps more important, they have been responsible for much of the offshore movement that has taken place in the more recent stages of development. Their overseas activities range from exploiting mineral and energy resources to the provision of financial services, from the setting up of branch plant factories to the operation of shipping lines.

The international dimension

Significant development appears to require interaction at an international level (i.e. internationalisation) (8.2). Certainly, no countries in the Asian Pacific region have achieved real development in isolation. Trade and overseas investment emerge as crucial factors. If these are to prosper, there must be a context of good international relationships and peace (i.e. geopolitics play their part). The big issue arising here is the nature of the relationship between any two nations. Is it one of dependence and inequality, in which the strong exploits the weak? Or is it one of true partnership, equality and interdependence? A third aspect of this dimension is the state of the global economy. This is of overriding importance.

The uniqueness of countries

The final point to be extracted from the case studies (it has already been implied) is a very geographical one: the uniqueness of countries and regions. Whilst we may like to make generalisations about the causes, nature and directions of development, it is only possible to do so within certain broad limits. Ultimately, no two countries are exactly alike. They will certainly differ in terms of the general level of development that has been reached at any moment in time. More important, though, their records will show significant differences in other vital aspects, such as the mechanisms generating development, as well as its precise nature and course. Equally, they will differ in terms of the social outcomes or benefits of development.

Hodder has put forward the idea that each country has a 'unique cultural signature' which profoundly moulds the character and direction of development. The 'signature' refers to 'the way people organise their economic, social and political life, and how they deal with the problems that arise. ... [It] is revealed in their aspirations, philosophies and attitudes; it involves their reactions to established views and forms or organisation, to new ideas and exotic stimuli; and it is in part a consequence of environment, history and chance events' (R. Hodder (1992) *The West Pacific Rim: An Introduction*, Belhaven). This feature needs to be added to our tentative model (**8.2**). It is shown as one of the ongoing outcomes.

Review

1 a Look at **4.11** and **8.2**. In what ways are they similar? How are they different?
  b Can you think of any ways in which **8.2** might be changed to make it a better model of development?

2 Discuss how and why the unique cultural signature of a country might affect the nature of its development. Support your views with examples.

SECTION B

Disparities in development – causes and cures

The factors outlined above also help to provide some sort of explanation for the spatial variations in development that occur between and within countries. Variations in development within countries are prominent in all the Asian Pacific states. Four related concepts may also help in completing the explanation – three are well-established in geographical studies, the fourth is possibly new (**8.3**).

The first is the concept of **initial advantage**. This relates to the greater benefits and momentum that come from being 'first in the field'. Once an 'advantage' or opportunity has been seized (it might be a particular resource, situation or technology), then the concept of **cumulative causation** becomes relevant. Processes set in that reinforce the competitiveness of the initial location and the benefits gained. A spatial situation of winners and losers is created – **cores** and **peripheries** emerge at national and regional scales. Equally, it has to be recognised that **stochastic processes** may well play a part. What this third concept suggests is that the initial location of development and the form it takes may be determined by chance; that is, by random circumstances that cannot be predicted with any certainty.

Perhaps not too far removed from the concepts of initial advantage and stochastic processes is the idea of **convergence (8.3)**. This concept is supported by the case histories of the Asian Pacific region's most successful economies – Japan, Hong Kong and Singapore. It involves an interaction of internal and external stimuli, as shown in **8.2**. In all three cases, successful development has been the outcome of a coming together – a marrying of human talents and determination, perceptive government and business enterprise to the opportunities created by changing external circumstances. For example, the opportunities offered by a particular phase in the evolution of the global economy and by a changing geopolitical situation. The latter gave particular strategic value to the locations of all three. In this context, location is to be seen as a resource.

Figure 8.3 Convergence and the creation of disparities

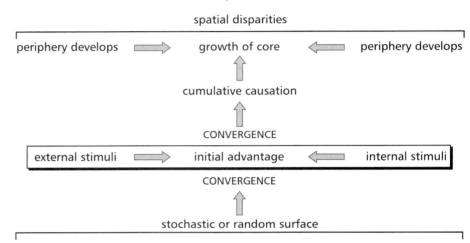

It is important to note that there is no even playing-field for the convergence which follows – there is no equal division of opportunities between nations; nor are nations equally able to seize those opportunities that happen to come their way **(8.3)**.

The commitment to reduce spatial disparities in development varies in time and space. At a national level, the wish to reduce the development gap between core and peripheral regions seems to intensify as development progresses. In some developed countries, it is clearly seen as the responsibility of government to close that gap by 'stick and carrot' measures. In others, there is the belief that market forces will eventually do the job, as Friedman's development model implies (**E & P 30.9**). The reluctance of governments of less-developed countries to intervene is understandable. Curbing growth in the core carries the risk of killing the goose that lays the golden egg.

When it comes to ironing out disparities at an international level, there is some contradiction. On the one hand, organisations such as the United Nations, the European Union and the World Bank, and charities like Oxfam, are committed to the principle of rich nations helping the poor. Although most of the wealthier nations give aid, at the same time they are doing everything they can to maintain, if not enhance, their own ranking in the development league-table. In a competitive world, this often may involve exploiting overseas resources and opportunities. By doing so they sustain a situation of dependency and inequality.

3 In your own words, explain the convergence idea.

4 Do you agree that 'disparities in development are inevitable and can never be completely cured'? Support your answer with examples.

One final point needs to be made. In a dynamic and upwardly mobile region such as the Asian Pacific region, a momentum builds up that may well bring wider benefits. It is possible that weaker and less-developed nations will be swept along by their stronger and more-developed neighbours in webs of dependence and interdependence. In this way, not only is there a trickling down of development, there is also the prospect of some reduction of development disparities. This may be of some comfort to the low-income economies.

SECTION C

Satisfaction and sustainability

A basic point made in **Chapter 1 Section B** was that this book has adopted a strongly economic view of development. Less searching attention has been given to the social, political, cultural and environmental outcomes of development in the Asian Pacific region (**1.1**).

The Human Development Index values in **8.4** suggest a reasonably close correlation with GNP per capita, with two obvious exceptions. First, there is the contrast within the lower middle income grouping between, on the one hand, Malaysia and Thailand, and on the other hand the Philippines and

Figure 8.4 Some social indicators of development in the Asian Pacific region (1992)

Economic grouping	Ranking based on GNP per capita	HDI	Adult literacy (%)	Expend. on education (% GNP)	Expend. on health (% GNP)	Population per doctor
High income	Japan	0.93	99	5	6.8	600
Higher middle income	Singapore	0.878	90	3.4	1.1	725
	Hong Kong	0.905	91	3.0	1.1	1100
	Taiwan	no data	93	3.6	no data	900
	Brunei	0.868	86	4.6	3.4	1500
	South Korea	0.882	97	3.6	2.7	1205
Lower middle income	Malaysia	0.822	82	6.9	1.3	2560
	Thailand	0.827	94	3.8	1.1	4760
	Phillipines	0.677	94	2.9	1.0	8330
	Indonesia	0.637	83	2.2	0.7	7140
Low income	China	0.594	79	2.3	2.1	1000
	Laos	0.420	54	1.1	1.0	4540
	Cambodia	0.337	38	no data	no data	9500
	Vietnam	0.539	92	3.0	1.1	250
	North Korea	0.733	95	3.7	no data	400

Indonesia; secondly there is the high index value for North Korea (are we seeing here an indication of 'massaged' statistics?). As for the other data, does it require much imagination to see some sort of broad relationship between the economic groupings and these measures of human progress and satisfaction? What we can be more certain about is the persistence of strong disparities. Look at the range in values under each of the five headings.

As to the sustainability of the economic progress that has been achieved in the region, what little evidence we have is distinctly pessimistic. For example, annual rates of deforestation between 1980 and 1995 showed that in five of the 15 Asian Pacific countries the rate was in excess of 1 per cent per annum. In another five countries the rate was between 0.5 and 1 per cent. In only four Asian Pacific countries were emissions of carbon dioxide in 1995 less than one tonne per capita. In Japan and North Korea the figures were eight and 11 tonnes respectively. Between 1970 and 1995 the production of energy in the Asian Pacific region increased by four times; natural gas output increased by 27 times and the production of cement by six times. Although Japan, the region's leader, has done much to improve the quality of its own environment, it remains a huge consumer of non-renewable resources. Much of the supply comes from dependent less-developed countries keen to cash in on their natural endowments.

This fragmented evidence of accelerating resource use and persistent pollution indicates that the Asian Pacific region has much to do in terms of 'greening' its development. The course of development so far in the region would appear to be a long way short of sustainability.

Review

5 a Calculate the rank correlations between **(i)** GNP per capita and each of the other measures in **8.4**, and **(ii)** each of the five social measures.

   b Write a brief account of your findings.

The way ahead

So, at the turn of the millennium, the Asian Pacific region is to be seen as an assemblage of diverse countries. Those countries are to varying degrees dependent and interdependent, but rarely pull together as parts of a unified whole. They show disparities with respect to standards of living and quality of life (**8.4**). Their development paths fall short of sustainability to varying degrees. Nonetheless, the progress achieved by its constituent countries has allowed the Asian Pacific region to consolidate its new-found status as a powerhouse of the global economy. Currently, it is unmatched in terms of the scale and pace of development taking place in most of its member countries. The balance of economic power in the North Pacific region tips increasingly towards the Asian rather than the American shore. Here there are two key players – Japan by virtue of its immense achievements and economic clout; China by virtue of its geographical enormity and awesome potential.

At the time of writing (December, 1997) many of the Asian Pacific countries are suffering from what has been termed 'Asian flu'. The symptoms are a sudden devaluation of currencies and collapse of stock markets, and a marked slowing down in rates of economic growth. The vital question is this – will the patient recover, or does this downturn mark the end of the Asian Pacific region's growth phase? There are four pointers that support the former scenario.

- Regular alternations of boom and bust are, and always have been, a characteristic of economic development at whatever scale – global, national or regional.
- The present downturn has been exaggerated by malpractices in the financial world. Banks, particularly in Japan and South Korea, have been overlending in an attempt to artifically boost development and make quicker and bigger profits. Eliminating this sort of speculation is going to be vital to the region's recovery. Firm goverment control of the private sector is perhaps called for.
- Although the economies of Japan and the four Tigers are now growing at slower rates, they still generate a huge annual output of absolute growth. Elsewhere in the region, there is still a vast reservoir of untapped development potential.
- There is no region in the world that currently threatens to rival the Asian Pacific region.

What has become quite clear is the contagious nature of the current crisis. What started in one or two countries has quickly spread not only to others in the region, but has rapidly impacted on the whole global economy. But this is to be expected, because all nations today – large or small, rich or poor – are bound together in a complex web of dependence and interdependence.

Looking to brighter times, there is one final question to be asked about the Asian Pacific region at the dawn of the 21st century. Should it follow Europe and set up some sort of economic-cum-political union. If it should do so, then an increase in interdependence might be one beneficial outcome, together with some reduction in the development disparities that currently divide member countries. But would such a union be able to deliver further significant overall development to match that achieved during the second half of the 20th century? And would it be able to ensure a 'greener', more sustainable mode of development?

With your fellow students, debate one of the following propositions:

- 'It is unreasonable to expect poorer countries to be concerned about the greening and sustainability of development.'

- 'Sustainable development: an unattainable ideal?'

- 'There is little to challenge the Asian Pacific region's status as the number one sunrise region.'

Further Reading and Resources

Further Reading

Chapman, G. P and Baker, K. M. (1993) *The Changing Geography of Asia* (Rouledge).

Hodder, R. (1992) *The West Pacific Rim: An Introduction* (Belhaven).

Drakakis-Smith, D. (1992) *Pacific Asia* (Routledge).

Dwyer, D. (ed.)(1990) *South-east Asia: geographical perspectives* (Longman).

Walters, R. F. and McGee, T. G. (1997) *New Geographies of the Pacific Rim – Asia Pacific* (Hurst).

Winchester, S. (1991) *The Pacific* (Hutchinson).

Witherick, M. and Carr, M. (1993) *The Changing Face of Japan* (Hodder & Stoughton).

World Bank (1993) *The East Asian Miracle* (OUP).

Zhao Songqiao (1994) *Geography of China* (Wiley).

Resources

The type of additional information needed for the Enquiries at the end of each chapter may often be found in the following sources:

Far Eastern Economic Review (weekly publication)

Financial Times (periodic national surveys)

Institute of Southeast Asian Studies (occasional publications)

Japan: An International Comparison (annual publication by Japan Insitute for Social and Economic Affairs)

National Reports (occasional publications by World Bank)

National web sites (or Stanley Thornes EPICS address) on the Internet

New Statesman Yearbook

Philip's Geographical Digest (annual publication by Heinemann)

The Economist (weekly publication)

World Bank Atlas (annual publication by World Bank)

World Bank Development Report (annual publication by World Bank)